The Kanga and the Kangaroo Court

The Kanga and the Kangaroo Court

Reflections on the Rape Trial of Jacob Zuma

Mmatshilo Motsei

Published by Jacana Media (Pty) Ltd in association
with Pinagare Media in 2007
Reprinted in 2007

10 Orange Street
Sunnyside
Auckland Park 2092
South Africa
(+27 11) 628-3200
www.jacana.co.za

ISBN 978-1-77009-255-6

Set in Ehrhardt 12/15pt
Printed by CTP Book Printers, Cape Town
Job No. 000437

See a complete list of Jacana titles at www.jacana.co.za

Contents

Silence is not an option

'I see a light
but no fire
is this what
my life is to be like
better to head for the grave'

Tagore

The Republic of South Africa (are we ever going to change this name?) is one great country. In 1994, 160 years after the abolition of slavery in the Cape Colony[1], the indigenous people of the land cast their vote for the very first time. A decade after that magical moment, the country had repealed and reversed some of the negative effects of brutal and draconian laws, as well as a history coloured by racial oppression. However, like a neophyte emerging from the mother's womb faced with the challenge of adapting to the real world, the country is faced with the challenge of balancing political and economic stability with a strong moral ethic as an integral part of national identity.

One good thing about the charade surrounding Jacob Zuma's trials is that it gives us an opportunity to stop and reflect as a nation. The trials present us with a crisis that enables us to look beyond the surface and ask searching questions about the meaning of justice, democracy and power. At stake, in this instance, is the question of political power. This power can be fickle and fragile. Here today, gone tomorrow. Because it is driven by a win or lose mentality, those who lose simply have to wait for a moment to avenge their loss, while those who win have a limited period of time during which they can display their popularity on public platforms. Conflict resolution is emotionally driven; many in Zuma's camp may be driven by their hate for President Mbeki's leadership style rather than their unwavering belief in Zuma's fitness to govern.

Asking deep fundamental questions about the way we govern cannot only be based on popular support. Neither can it only depend on the power of the intellect. It must also be founded on our ability to feel. This means we cannot only rely on the logic of the mind but must also rely on higher logic that brings the heart to the question of leadership. Bringing the heart to governance implies governing in a way that generates the greatest good for the greatest number of people. According to Lorraine Canoe, a Mohawk Indian leader, a powerful leader is one who has the ability to put politics in one hand, the spirit in the other, and then bring them together.[2] Such politics, according to Canoe, is transformational because it embodies personal and social change.

For South Africa, the pursuit of transformational politics demands a conscious regeneration and reintegration of our moral values into our policies. However, regeneration of our morality in a capitalist society driven by a 'what do I stand to gain?' mentality as opposed to 'what's at stake for the country?' is a constant battle of harmonising the spirit with the heart and head.

When he delivered the JD Baqwa Memorial Lecture at the University of Cape Town in 2006, rector of the University of South Africa, Prof. Barney Pityana, referred to the remarks about the growing consumerist and materialist nature of our society made by President Mbeki in his Nelson Mandela Lecture at Wits University on 29 July 2006. In his lecture, Prof. Pityana outlined the emerging world of South Africa's *nouveau riches* who are engrossed in the dog-eat-dog, cut-throat world of black economic empowerment (BEE) deals. Such a world, he argued, makes no room for quality of life or family life. The ultimate outcome, he argued, is a breakdown of moral values fuelled by greed, corruption and criminal activity.[3]

For a nation emerging from a protracted war that required numbing of the soul and hardening of the heart to achieve political liberation, an awakening of the spirit embedded in the ancient African philosophy of *phela ke phele* (live and let live) is one of the greatest challenges for leaders and the nation as a whole. Indeed, one of the most important questions facing us is: can the revival and reintegration of this principle into our lives solve the current state of moral decay? If the answer is yes, how can this be done?

In his monograph *Current Perspectives on Afrikan Philosophy*, Dr Kgalushi Koka tells a story about an American Catholic bishop, the Rev. Fulton Sheen, who visited Europe in 1957 and stopped in Johannesburg on his way home, conducting a Holy Mass at St. Pius Church in Mofolo Village, Soweto. In his sermon, Rev. Sheen remarked that at the time when the East and West were at each other's throats during the Cold War, Africa would save these countries from mutual destruction through its revival and application of a philosophy of humanness or *ubuntu*.[4]

The application of *ubuntu* is, however, not limited to religion and should therefore not only be housed in religious institutions. Rather, it should be explored within the deeper realms of spirituality inherent in all people. In his essay 'I Am Because We Are', esteemed African son of the soil Eskia Mphahlele relates a story told by a Bengali poet, Rabindranath Tagore, of a song from a beggar who belonged to a Bengali sect called the Baul.[5] In the song, Tagore described an intense yearning of the heart for that which is divine in man and not in the temple, scriptures or symbols. According to Mphahlele, African humanism, like traditional Indian thought, emphasises the longing to *be*, rather than to *have*.

> *'The traditional African has shrines but not churches or temples, and his faith in the Supreme Being finds expression in social relationships, in music, in his art and craftwork, in the cultivation of the soil, and so on. To meet the eternal spirit in all objects and all humans is to be emancipated. Our ancestral spirits teach us through proverb, folktale, and song the wisdom on how to conduct ourselves in order to realize the Supreme Being as a Vital Force in all our relationships with things and beings.'* [6]

Ubuntu is an ancient philosophy founded on the notion of communalism, *motho ke motho ka batho* (I am because we are), driven by attributes such as truth, justice and compassion. This philosophy does not discriminate on the grounds of race, economic affluence, social status or gender. It is a flow of life that is the same for every member of the human race. *Ubuntu* is not only tied to human life. It also concerns itself with respect for animals and the environment. The adoption of such a philosophy therefore seeks to create a balance between the self and others, as well as between the internal and external.

Ubuntu is a philosophy that could assist in rebuilding unity within and amongst different communities. However, healing can only occur when the wounds of the past are reopened and understood. People who undertake this journey are sometimes accused of being stuck in the past.

In my book *Hearing Visions Seeing Voices*, I alluded to the fact that forgiveness should not be used to force black people to forget the past.[7] This means that for black people, proving that they have healed and that they practise *ubuntu* does not mean they should agree with external prescriptions on who and how to forgive, or why and when, without coming to terms with the extent of their suffering in their own way, in their own time. At the same time, black people should avoid being stuck in pain and rage, a place that has the potential to make them serve time in a prison that has no walls. This will obliterate efforts to kill the enemy within by liberating their hearts from the heavy burden of hatred and a quest for revenge.

Fighting the enemy within our hearts and minds is a personal liberation required for the fundamental racial, economic and moral transformation of society. Because transformation is personal work, a regeneration of moral values that fosters *ubuntu* or *botho* neither is a movement of the Presidency, nor does it belong to the masses. It is about the individual. An individual contribution to it includes confronting our sense of entitlement to a position or a contract because of our political affiliation, struggle credentials, educational qualifications, class privilege, race or gender. My contribution involves taking a stand against buying stolen goods and against all forms of discrimination and oppression, greed and corruption. A revolution based on truth and justice starts with me.

Zuma, moral regeneration and sexual violence
No-one seemed to understand the depth and breadth of the challenges of moral leadership other than Jacob Zuma himself. In opening the first Moral Regeneration Movement (MRM) conference in Midrand in November 2004, Zuma challenged people to focus on building a caring, humane and ethical society.

> *'The MRM was founded on the principles that South Africans are highly moral beings, know the difference between right and wrong, and are appalled by the*

symptoms of moral decay which sometimes occur in our country. These include blatant disregard for the sanctity of human life, the abuse of women and children, crime, substance abuse, lack of respect for the next person and their property and so forth.' [8]

In his address, the then deputy president went on to outline that the issues raised above were critical elements in the government's five-year plan. He also reiterated the MRM's commitment to the fight against Aids, 'especially with regards to promoting a change in behaviour, which would greatly assist the campaign to reduce new infections'.

Four years later, we know very little about the achievements of the Moral Regeneration Movement. What we know for sure is that a champion and driver of the movement was charged with rape after having sex without a condom with a woman living with HIV. During his trial, Zuma maintained that he was HIV negative. This means that making a conscious decision to have unprotected sex with a woman openly living with the virus was not in line with the campaign to reduce new infections.

In yet another address on the occasion of World Aids Day at Athlone Stadium in Cape Town on 1 December 2004, Zuma emphasised the need to focus on women's empowerment as a foundation for achieving equality in gender relations in the private and public spheres. According to him, women were still vulnerable to men's greater economic and social power, which affects their ability to negotiate safer sex. As a result, many women are left with little or no control over their exposure to the virus. In his concluding comments, Zuma urged everyone to take the message of HIV prevention seriously.

'The action of each person counts in this war against Aids. If everybody takes the messages of abstention, faithfulness or condom use [ABC] seriously and acts

> *on it, we can achieve our goal of drastically reducing*
> *the rate of infections.'* [9]

If one thing is clear from Zuma's utterances in court, it is that HIV/Aids prevention is not as easy as the concept of ABC. In one sense, ABC is largely focused on individual risk without considering how broader contextual factors affect an individual's access to information, his interpretation of the information in relation to his own world view, his motivation to act, as well as his ability or inability to act within existing cultural, economic and other external norms that govern his behaviour.

Clearly, in Zuma's situation, abstinence (A) is totally out question for a married polygamist who has publicly admitted to having sex with a woman who is not his regular partner. As far as B and C are concerned, he chose to be neither faithful (B), nor to use a condom (C). When he responded to a question regarding his reasons for not using a condom, he was reported to have said it was because he knew that, as a man, he has a low risk of contracting the virus. In this way, he conveniently chose to forget one of the greatest cornerstones of African life; a person is a person through others, meaning what you do has direct impact on others. This fact is reinforced by an African–American psychiatrist, Dr Frances Cress Welsing, who argues in her book *The Isis Papers* that 'behavior is not simply an individual affair, for when multiplied by thousands, it has profound effects on the life, future existence and well-being of a total people'.[10]

If one was to multiply Zuma's utterances in court about women, sex and HIV with his multitudes of supporters converging on the courts in Johannesburg and Pietermaritzburg and the supporters at the public rallies he addressed, the overall impact on the psyche of a nation will be catastrophic not only to the living but to the unborn. If all his male supporters choose to have sex without a condom because 'they know that they have a slim chance of contracting the virus' the outcome will be dire.

Minister of Social Development Dr Zola Skweyiya's efforts in supporting Aids orphans would be tantamount to pouring money into a bottomless pit.

As a married man, Zuma chose not to care about the effect of his actions on his sexual partners irrespective of whether they were regular or not. It is such thinking that is behind many men's attitudes to sex with women. Once aroused, some men prefer instant release at the expense of long-term health and longevity. In many such instances, a sexually aroused man will persuade, cajole, or even force himself on a woman irrespective of whether a condom is available or not. Often, if and when a condom is negotiated, it is the man who will ultimately agree to use it and keep it on during the entire act of intercourse. This makes the male condom an unreliable way of preventing the spread of HIV and Aids. We know from women's experiences that many who contracted HIV did so in monogamous relationships.

UBaba Gedleyihlekisa Zuma is not a young man. His decision to engage in 'consensual sex' with a woman other than his regular partners was not the uninformed and risky behaviour of a boy who is still experimenting with sex. It was definitely not the decision of a young man who finally has a 'stadium' and a chance to 'grab some hasty pussy' and who later returns to the street corner to brag about his conquest to his peers. This was the action of an elder and a father of children who are the same age as his one-night stand.

As a respected elder in his community and an astute politician who once chaired the South African National Aids Council, he was well aware of the consequences of a decision to have sex with a woman young enough to be his daughter who is not only HIV positive but who, because of historical and cultural reasons, holds him in awe. He was aware of the power he held over her; he knew that in spite of Judge Van der Merwe's failure to grasp an expansive notion of family that goes beyond blood lineage, he was a father-figure to her and had a moral obligation to exercise control over his sexual urges, especially if and when sex was initiated by her. As someone who has a keen eye and ear for tradition, he is aware of the principle of 'my child is your child, your child is mine' which, in African societies, encourages biological and non-biological parents to take communal responsibility for the material, psychological and moral well-being of every child in their community.

Because of his strong belief in ancestors, Zuma must have known that the wrath of the spirit of his comrade who died in exile leaving behind a distraught ten-year-old daughter might come back to haunt him. As a former head of intelligence in the ANC, he must have been trained to be highly suspicious of untoward sexual attention, especially at the time when he was allegedly facing a political conspiracy to oust him from the presidential succession race. Despite all this, his training and experience in political intelligence, being an elder, husband, father and a leader purporting to uphold traditional values, Zuma chose to have unprotected sex with the complainant. Political conspiracy or not, his choice to engage in sex was in his hands alone.

It was his hands that lowered the kanga and massaged her with baby oil; it had nothing to do with the invisible hand of a third force. It was his hands that turned her body around and his fingers that were inserted into her vagina; it had nothing to do with political camps. It was his arms that held her as he penetrated her; it had nothing to do with the arms deal. It was his hand that he raised in court swearing to tell nothing but the truth. It is indeed his hand that he may use to sign the document in 2009 after being sworn in as the leader of one of the most powerfully evolving nations in the southern hemisphere. The choice between 10 minutes of instant gratification and 10 years in the highest office of the land was his and his alone. After all, there is no greater power than the power of choice.

However, what Zuma did cannot be condemned in isolation. It is a reflection of the prevailing thoughts, attitudes and perceptions in broader society. Not many men and women can claim to have been completely faithful to their partners. Similarly, not all people who are faced with the risk of HIV use condoms all the time. Likewise, Zuma is not the only leader whose hands are contaminated by accepting bribes. We know from various media reports that fraud and corruption is a cancer spreading its roots in our government, business and the country at large.

Corruption in South Africa is not a new phenomenon. We know from history that the apartheid regime used state money for political and personal purposes. It is a well-known fact that good and ethical governance is not a phrase that could be used to describe the previous racist regime. Similarly, we know from various scandals in governments across the world that fraud and corruption are not only confined to Africa or black governments. It is my view that black governments would need to stoop very low (ethically speaking) to match imperialist and racist regimes in the world.

We cannot condone these actions because 'everyone else is doing it'. It is important to search for solutions that will ensure that common vices do not become common virtues. As we engage in self-examination through campaigns such as the Truth and Reconciliation Commission, the Moral Regeneration Movement and the Batho Pele campaign, to name a few, are we ready for honest and full examination or are we bent on condemning others while we know full well that their actions mirror our own hidden thoughts and beliefs? Considering the extent of moral decay and gross expressions of inhumanity that exist in contrast to the celebrated economic boom, perhaps it's time to reflect on what the Chinese sage Confucius once said: 'When we see men of a contrary character, we should turn inwards and examine ourselves.'

The response to Zuma's rape charges as demonstrated by his supporters is a reflection of moral double standards that are applied differently to women and men. Let's assume that Jacob Zuma was a woman for a moment, let's call her Jacobeth.

Jacobeth is a rural woman of 64, married with children. She is one of the stalwarts of liberation in South Africa who left the country in her youth to play a meaningful role in the activities of the African National Congress. She was also one of the first women who returned to the country to pave the way for negotiations and peace in a country riddled by violence and war. As one of the key women in the country, she is well respected by all.

She is a warrior against any form of injustice; she works tirelessly and speaks out openly against poverty, especially in rural areas. Because of her commitment to a better life for all, she has established a bursary scheme to confront lack of access to education for young people in her village and beyond. She is a selfless Mother of the Nation. It is an open secret that she is tipped to become the next president.

Because of her dedication and the demands of her work, she is forced to spend time away from her husband and children. On one of her nights away from home, she was visited by a young man well known to the family, a son whose mother was Jacobeth's close friend and comrade in exile. The young man, aged 31, held her in awe and loved her as a mother. On that night, the two had sex.

If the young man reported a case of rape, how would we respond to the allegations? Who would we accuse of being at fault? What names would we use to describe Jacobeth? How would her husband react to the news? What would people say about her husband's reaction? Would there be any chanting of 'shoot the motherfucker' to express outrage towards a promiscuous 'son of a bitch' for seducing the mother of the nation? If any underwear was burnt outside the court, would it be a man's underwear or would we be burning the panties of an old bitch and cradle-snatcher who exposed herself unashamedly to a man young enough to be her son? If she accepted her wrongdoing and apologised to the nation for her act, would she be forgiven? If not, why not?

It was on waking up to the headline 'Burn the Bitch' at Jacob Zuma's rape trial on International Women's Day, 8 March 2006, twelve years into South Africa's new democracy, ten years after the implementation of the new Constitution and fifty years after women marched to the Union Buildings to demand their rights, that the pervasive disrespect for women and women's rights was brought home.

For me personally, Jacob Zuma's rape trial was both a form of victimisation and a moment of reawakening. Seeing him arrive in court and being ushered in with ceremonial pomp surrounded by an army of bodyguards in dark suits leaping out of a motorcade of luxury automobiles and running towards the court building, I wondered if Thomas Jefferson was correct when he said 'A people get a government they deserve'.

I know from talking to other people that the South African political landscape will never be the same again. I also know from reading what many women and men wrote about the trial, including its outcome, that the experience had a shocking impact on the nation. Like the complainant, many of us were deeply affected by the experience.

Painful and confusing as it was, a handful of courageous women and men spoke out and seized the moment as an opportunity to revisit ways in which women's freedoms can be repressed in democratic societies. For those of us who have been part of a painful and vibrant movement that ensured that women's equality is enshrined in the Constitution, silence is not an option. We know from the experiences of women in post-colonial nations that even when they have fought alongside their men, after liberation, they are expected to return to the kitchen and bedroom. We know from women's experience all over the world that violence, including rape, is a weapon used to 'put women in their place'.

Faced with an ever-increasing prevalence of rape and other forms of violence against women in South Africa, we are challenged like never before to revisit deeply buried stereotypes that inform our views of women in relation to men (e.g. a woman can never lead, she is inferior or evil) in the same way we confront our hidden view of blacks in relation to whites (*setlhare sa mosotho ke lekgoa* – black people are inferior, violent and stupid). Just as racism increases the potential of violence against black people, sexism has a similar effect on women.

Unlike racism, however, sexist practices are perpetrated not only by strangers but also by those with whom women live intimately. The fact that the home is one of the institutions in society that reinforce deeply entrenched sexist beliefs presents a major challenge to efforts aimed at rooting out sexism. It is in the home that some of the most brutal forms of violence and torture are perpetrated against those perceived to be weak, i.e. women and children. It is no wonder that a greater proportion of women who are raped are violated not by strangers but by someone they know and trust in the 'safety' of their own homes. Contrary to popular belief, the home is not necessarily a safe place for women and children.

Societal responses to rape in South Africa

The escalating rate of sexual violence in South Africa is alarming. The increasing occurrence of rape is not only worrying; the fact that the assaults are also accompanied by vicious sadism and gross mutilation of women's bodies is of deep concern. The use of knives and guns during rape is commonplace as are the harrowing accounts of women being penetrated by foreign objects such as bottles.

Many women's organisations reveal that most incidents of sexual violence go unreported. We know from the recent 1 in 9 campaign that for every woman who reports rape, nine others are silenced by fear, shame and guilt. The one woman who has the courage to report a rape has to recount her experience in graphic detail to secure a conviction. This person who has suffered the trauma of one of the most horrendous crimes imaginable has to present her ordeal in a rational and logical manner. Furthermore, she also has to show that she is not of loose moral character otherwise her case will be disadvantaged by past sexual experiences, which may have no bearing on her current claim. In many ways, the accuser is cast as the accused.

> *'She should have screamed if this was really rape. Even with a gun, you have to come out of that without being raped. Even if he slaps you – you run away, you scream, you do whatever you can do to stop him.'* [11]

This is the voice of a woman interviewed outside the Johannesburg High Court during Jacob Zuma's rape trial. It is founded on the belief that a woman who fails to show visible injuries as a sign of having resisted rape may have engaged in sex willingly. How and how much should she resist? Very often, those who do resist end up being beaten mercilessly and raped repeatedly. To secure a conviction, does a woman have to present evidence of a breast slashed with a knife or a vagina stuffed with sand? What about a woman raped by a man who whispers sweet nothings in her ear as he thrusts violently, working himself to a state of temporary insanity?

The supporter quoted above was of the opinion that the complainant ruined her hero's political career and therefore deserved to be condemned in the strongest possible manner. As a woman, she is expected to have prevented her attack by fighting him off. If we compare this to a hijacking, we find that potential victims are advised not to fight back but to hand over their car keys to the hijacker without any struggle, to avoid injury. This is irrespective of whether the hijacker and the victim are both strong men. Similarly, whilst laying a charge of robbery at a police station, a business owner is never quizzed to find out whether he fought back or if he quietly submitted to the ordeal. Evidence of fighting the robber by shouting, screaming or getting physical is not required as a precondition for laying a charge or the payment of an insurance claim.

A woman who is immobilised by fear may not be physically strong enough to fend off her rapist. In addition to being physically injured, or even murdered, a woman who is raped is presumed to be guilty by society if she does not fight back. Furthermore, she is also blamed for being born female. This means that she not only has to contend with the trauma of sexual violence, she also has to face a deep, negative social stigma that surrounds womanhood, sex and sexual violence.

Narrations of the impact of the stigma of rape are found in many works of fiction and non-fiction. In her novel *And They Didn't Die*, Lauretta Ngcobo outlines the shame felt by Jezile, a woman from Umzimkhulu who was raped by her employer. Of concern to her was not only that she was raped but the reality that she would be accused of bringing the name of Siyalo, her husband, as well as his family into disrepute.

> '*Panic and horror seized her. He had her arm twisted and he rolled her onto the bed and pinned her down... He had his way with her... He did not leave the room when he had finished with her... He sat up next to her trying to calm her down and to comfort her. "If it wasn't for the law, I would love you openly; I would even marry you." Finally he left the room after midnight. She felt dirty and steeped in evil. The feel and the smell of his slimy emission filled her with much revulsion... But as dawn broke, the thought of telling her community back in Sigageni about her*

bitter experience filled her with shame. She was no longer sure of their sympathy and understanding... something in her could not face it. Rape is a burden to its own victim. It was as though she had wished it on herself. She could predict all the lurid gossip... And what would Siyalo think when he came back and heard these stories? Would he believe her against all those rumours?' [12]

A woman I met during my work in Alexandra Township was raped by two young men and had to face the wrath of her husband, who accused her of asking for it.

'My husband did not come home that night. Very early the next day, at about 5am, I left the house to go and look for him. I had to go because if he gets injured I will have to answer to my in-laws. They might accuse me of not being a good wife. As I walked past the women's hostel, two young men approached me and dragged me to some part of the hostel threatening me with a knife on my neck. I tried to fight; they assaulted me with a fist and later raped me. After they had left, I went back home to wait for my husband. On arrival, I told him what happened. He was very angry with me, accusing me of following him around. He shouted at me saying that I asked for it because I was supposed to have stayed at home like a good wife until he comes back.' [13]

Women's experiences of the trauma of rape begin early in their lives. Given the prevalence of the sexual abuse of children, many women have guilt-ridden childhood memories of bearing the brunt of misogynistic violence directed to those who are born female. Similarly, there are very few women who have not experienced a lover forcing himself on them. There aren't many who do not have a memory of coerced sexual intercourse, which is reactivated by forceful sexual acts with regular partners. If this is a disease, then thousands, millions, of women are ill. If the complainant in Zuma's rape trial is ill, her disease does not exist in a vacuum but in a society where men do not think twice about descending on a woman's body like a pack of vultures feasting on a dead carcass. Indeed, if she is pronounced ill, Zuma must also be ill. Just like the complainant who might, according to Judge Van der Merwe, 'perceive any sexual encounter as rape', Zuma might perceive all acts of patriarchal sex as consensual.

Women were not born ill. Their socialisation as girls in a society structured by patriarchal attitudes is the root cause of the disease. Through an organised tyranny of religion, tradition, political, legal and economic systems, women's minds have been constrained and their bodies violated without consent. Confronted by the conspiracy of silence, women had to learn to accept that there must be 'something wrong in their drawers'[14] and that they would suffer for being born female. Against all odds, those in positions of power (including marital and blood male relatives) hoped that women would keep silent and never find a voice to question these repressive systems.

> *'I have never been free from the fear of rape. From a very early age, I, like most women, have thought of rape as part of my natural environment – something to be feared and prayed against like fire or lightning...*
>
> *At the age of eight my grandmother took me to the back of the house where men wouldn't hear, and told me that strange men wanted to harm little girls. I learned not to walk on dark streets, not to talk to strangers, or get into strange cars, to lock doors, and to be modest. She never explained why a man would want to harm a little girl, and I never asked.'* [15]

Rape goes far beyond a man penetrating a woman's vagina with his penis. It is, according to Kalamu ya Salaam, an act of denying women the autonomy of self-determination in the same way that the imperialists usurped the sovereignty of colonised nations.[16] Depending on who the victim is and who the rapist is, Ya Salaam argues that rape becomes an expression of the ideologies of racism, capitalism and sexism. Therefore, rape cannot be divorced from the objectification of women in the media, commercials, music videos, billboards and the pages of glossy magazines.

Running through the commercialised and misogynist depiction of women is the message that they are men's property. As a result, sex becomes a commodity that men consume rather than something that women and men share together. This explains the common notion of *re ja bana or re ja khekhe*, which runs as a thread through men's conversations about women and sex. This notion of *chowing the babes* exists despite the man being the one who surrenders to the 'little death', losing his essence to a woman while she retains her essence (and his) within her body.

Ending sexual violence against women goes far beyond legislation. It requires a change in societal attitudes through comprehensive community education campaigns on gender violence and its impact on women, families and communities. Early in 1995 I was appointed as a gender consultant in the Presidency and tasked with overseeing the process of formulating women's empowerment policies in the new democracy. My team focused its energies on establishing the National Gender Machinery and protective legislation such as the Domestic Violence Act. More than a decade later, appropriate gender institutions are in place, policies have been formulated and legislation has been passed, but thousands of women remain prisoners of war in their own homes and country.

Clearly, as far as the substance of the law is concerned, there are limitations to what it can do. It gives women certain rights and prescribes appropriate forms of punishment if these rights are violated. The laws may change but unless the attitudes of judges, lawyers, the police and other members of society change, the impact of new legislation will be limited. Urgent calls to pass the Sexual Offences Bill should also be accompanied by calls for the widespread legal education of women. Such an education should include a comprehensive public awareness campaign that eliminates the socio-cultural myths that perpetuate rape in our society.

Educating the public about their legal rights cannot be limited only to the written word in a language that not everyone understands. Given that about three million adults in South Africa are completely illiterate, between five and eight million are functionally illiterate and ten million are aliterate, such an educational campaign should occur within a context that is culturally relevant for the target population.[17] Otherwise, lengthy public lectures such as the one that Judge Van der Merwe gave when he allowed the complainant's sexual history to be taken into consideration in the Zuma case will not only be meaningless but could also prove to be dangerous since their misinterpretation could fuel the raging fire of sexual violence in South Africa. Some men might read women's humiliation during cross-examination about their sexual history as tacit approval for men to dominate women sexually – it gives men permission to blame women for rape.

The politics of rape

Undoubtedly, the greatest weapon in this battle is organising and recruiting women, men and entire communities to be part of a struggle that exposes the links between sexism and racism. A need to heal relationships between black women and men is

25

of critical importance. Focusing on black men is, however, not meant to reinforce the common myth of black men being violent by nature. It is meant, rather, to bring attention to the abuse they suffered for centuries.

One of the most calculated and premeditated forms of rape in Africa occurred in the 19th century when King Leopold II and other European monarchs rationalised their immoral acts of rape and plunder of Africa's human and natural resources as bringing civilization to parts of the globe whose darkness has not yet been penetrated by the white man's enlightenment. The legacy of such enlightenment is well recorded in history – the brutality of the Germans in Namibia, the Belgians in the Congo, the English and the Dutch in South Africa, the Portuguese in Mozambique, and the Italians in Somalia – the list goes on. European countries small enough to fit into a geographical space equivalent to Gauteng have perfected the art of exploiting vast continents such as Africa, Asia and Latin America. Indigenous peoples across the world are still suffering the trauma of foreign invasion.

Similarly, focusing on black men is also not meant to reinforce the myth of the black man as a rapist. It is not intended to turn a blind eye to the rape of black women by white men. We know from history that while slave owners had unrestricted access to slave women's bodies, they viewed black men as sexual predators who possessed an insatiable appetite for white women. For this reason, they felt a need to exert tight patriarchal control over white women's bodies as a way of protecting them from black rapists.[18] In its 1872 congressional report, the Ku Klux Klan required its initiates to take an oath to protect white women from black rapists. This protection was used as justification for the lynching of black people in America's southern states.[19]

The same was true of the Cape Colony where rape served as a rite of passage for young settler men. In writing about the life of Sarah Baartman, Yvette Abrahams reports that institutionalised rape was so embedded in the settler culture to the point where a white man's death sentence for raping a woman was reversed when evidence revealed that the victim was not white but Khoekhoe.[20]

Similarly, in her book *Women, Race and Class* Angela Davis argues that rape laws were originally framed to protect upper-class men. What happened to working-class black women was of no concern to the courts. As a result, the rape charge was indiscriminately aimed at black men. Of the 455 men executed on the basis of rape convictions between 1930 and 1967 in the United States, 405 of them were black.[21]

The image of the black man as rapist is, according to Angela Davis, inseparable from the notion of black women as chronically promiscuous. If it is accepted that black men 'are ravishers of white women', black women must welcome the sexual attention of white men.[22]

Furthermore, the notion of black men as rapists is based on a racist view of black men as sex maniacs derived from biological and sociological stereotypes coined by a range of theorists and scientists. By 'peeping' into the lives of black men in the ghetto, observing their behaviour like a scientist studying a group of chimpanzees in a cage, some of these scientists reduced their subjective observations to biological make-up and/or environmental effects. These theories assume that black men can't help raping women because they are born that way, or because they are raised to behave in this way. In contrast, however, the stories of victims of other atrocities such as the Holocaust are narrated not as stories of learned helplessness but as tales of triumph demonstrating the power of the human condition to transcend genetic and/or environmental limitations.

As a people, we have internalised these stereotypical notions of black men's sexuality.

Although they shocked us, it came as no surprise to hear Jacob Zuma's remarks about Zulu culture and rape. For many of us it was a reminder of ways in which the white man's misinterpretation of African custom was assisted by and contributed to black men's manipulation of tradition to perpetuate male domination. Traditional customs that pertain to women's sexual behaviour are often presented as rigid constructs of our past that can neither be changed nor challenged.

The tendency for people to exploit tradition for a particular purpose is commonplace in modern society. Its success rests on an appeal to 'go back to our roots', which for men who were dehumanised by oppressive regimes seems to be the only way to resist further dehumanisation by feminism, which they believe has foreign origins.

The growth of feminist scholarship, including its attack on nationalist agendas that uphold leadership principles espoused by elite men, has invoked counterattacks that see African feminists as vehicles for cultural contamination. In this instance, Desiree Lewis argues, culture is used to silence women and to keep them in an inferior position.

> *'Fictions of undiluted African culture have been weapons for enforcing women's obedience, with the charge of "Westernisation" being used against many women in public realms dominated by men. Women so castigated are pressurised to modify their "untraditional" behaviour or relinquish an identity that appears to bequeath a communal identity. Yet the selective lauding of certain institutions, customs or values lays bare the spuriousness of discourses that claim to speak in the name of culture.'* [23]

When I saw Zulu men in court on judgment day proudly displaying their African identity in a society that tried to crush the spirits of their ancestors for years, listening to them sing in their mother tongue as their hero received judgment in a foreign language from a system founded on the colonial ideology of European law, I wondered what it meant to be a man in a contemporary African society. Does King Goodwill Zwelithini's view of being a man differ fundamentally from that of King Shaka? If it does, how does it differ? Are the standards of being a man in Africa only measured within the confines of tribal beliefs, or can they be judged by something that transcends being Zulu or Sotho, or belonging to the Shembe, Muslim or Christian faiths?

Invariably, any attempt to answer these questions reminds us of the brutal impact apartheid had on our psyches. While it is important to revert back to our past to find healing, it is also critical that we confront the malignancy of violent crime in our communities.

> *'While it may be relevant now to talk about black in relation to white, we must not make this our preoccupation, for it can be a negative exercise. As we proceed further towards the achievement of our goals let us talk more about ourselves and our struggle and less about whites.'* [24]

For a long time the struggle was about fighting an external enemy. Now that we have attained democratic rule, how do we learn to fight for our souls? Fighting for, as opposed to fighting against, calls for a critical, self-loving and inward-looking review of ourselves. However, while the review is contextualised in the pain of our past, it needs to focus not only on our self-destructive natures but also on our abilities to transcend our violent past.

With regard to gender equality, is it possible for women to speak honestly to each other and to men? To be successful such encounters will require intense self-critique. Not all men are gender insensitive. Similarly, not all women are gender conscious. If they have been raised in a patriarchal culture, women are capable of being abusive. Because of their emotional and linguistic abilities, women are prone to abusing others verbally and emotionally. Verbal abuse can be as devastating as physical abuse; harsh words can be as deadly as a bullet.

While women focus on confronting widespread male violence, it is equally important that they stay alert to the subtle ways they may collude with patriarchy. For instance, how many times do women refer to one another as 'bitch', especially when fighting over a man? Women might rebel against men who refer to them as bitches and whores, yet refer to another woman in the same way. In a rural gender and HIV/Aids programme that I was a part of in Burgersfort, Limpopo Province, women constantly referred to other women as *kwababane* (whore). The greatest challenge for us was to show the women how internalised oppression (racism and sexism) controls their oppressed sense of self and identity.

For instance, a common belief that a woman cannot lead a country explains why other women obstruct gender equality by refusing to vote for or support the efforts of a capable woman leader. I was fascinated by a photograph of a woman wearing ANC colours outside the court buildings carrying a placard bearing a bold message: NO WOMAN PRESIDENT. This self-discrimination and negative self-image is not a 'woman thing'. It is a human phenomenon. Often the oppressed internalise and come to believe the oppressor's negative view of themselves explaining it as 'this is how black people are' or 'this is how women are'.

In many ways, some of the actions of women supporters outside the court buildings during Jacob Zuma's trial illustrate this fact. How else do you explain an image of a self-respecting elderly African woman burning *impepho* (cleansing herbs) in one hand and holding a G-string in the other, calling for the ancestors' intervention whilst cursing in words that, according to Don Makatile, make 'bitch' seem like a tame Sunday school word? How else do you explain such vile expressions of self-hate from older African women in the presence of young men who look to them for moral education? Was there no way of showing support for Msholozi without vilifying women's bodies?

Actions of support outside the court buildings not only reinforced the belief of women as temptresses, they also went further to reinforce the view of male revolutionaries as sex symbols. The same applies to cultural icons. From Che Guevara to Steve Biko, Bill Clinton to Bin Laden, Fela Kuti to Miles Davis, Bob Marley to Tupac, George Burns to Hugh Hefner, industry (sex, politics, religion, show business, media, etc.) markets power as an aphrodisiac, which makes women hover around these men like moths around a flame. Essentially, any man with power – money, muscle, fame, political popularity or intellectual wit – seems to be allowed to juggle as many women as he can.

In such instances, women play a stereotypical role of 'hot sex on a platter'.[25] Even ANC Chief Whip Mbulelo Goniwe is reported to have used his position of power to try to get a parliamentary office assistant to have sex with him. When the woman refused, Goniwe was allegedly reported to have said: 'I thought you were a real Xhosa girl. How can you say "no" to your chief whip as if I am an ordinary man?'[26]

Combining a view of men's power as an aphrodisiac with women's negative sense of self, some women openly accused the complainant of being ungrateful for an opportunity to have had sex with Msholozi. MaMkhize, an ardent supporter from Umzimkhulu who achieved celebrity status during the trial, stated that if she had been raped by Zuma she would not have bathed her bosom (where he'd have lain) for days.[27]

Dismantling patriarchal thinking and practice therefore goes beyond a female empowerment strategy that only focuses on putting women in powerful positions. It involves confronting the culture of patriarchal thinking that can be found in men as easily as it can be found in women. In a country where most families are headed by women, to what degree do single mothers force their sons to conform to patriarchal standards in their relationships with their girlfriends and wives?

For men, self-examination includes asking key questions: is it possible for men to live life-affirming, fulfilling and meaningful lives without dominating women? If you take away a man's ability to have sex with a woman, provide for the family and dominate social institutions, is he still a man? What makes a man a man? How is the identity and role of men in contemporary society affected by modern pressures? How does pressure to perform in a boardroom translate into pressure to perform in a bedroom? Does the existing widespread feeling of men's impotence (sexual and social) signify failure of the male machine gun?

According to Kalamu ya Salaam, it is not women's quest for independence that should become the central problem. Rather, Ya Salaam argues, men of African descent must examine their own impotence in contemporary culture.

> *'If we didn't have women to beat on, to pimp off, to massage our egos, to treat us like the kings we desire to be but aren't, to stand behind us when no-one else in the world would even think of us, what would we have to do?'* [28]

As far as parenting is concerned, do men have a greater and more significant role in child development other than providing for their material needs? In their absence, who is helping boys to decipher images of misogynist violence acted out in contemporary popular culture? Where are the fathers and father figures when boys act out in response to their unasked and unanswered questions through drugs and violence?

In most countries, men's average incomes are higher than women's and they control the tools of violence in the form of weapons and armed forces. Within the corporate sector, men have greater control of wealth. In South Africa, however, we cannot talk about male privilege without addressing the legacy of racial discrimination reflected in the high levels of poverty and unemployment amongst black men. Until such time that black men triumph over the social conditions that force them to participate in their own massacre, we cannot claim to be free. Political freedom without economic empowerment is a hollow victory. However, economic empowerment without spiritual emancipation is not only hollow but deadly.

Currently, many black men's bodies are rotting in jail (as they did during apartheid) and their minds are slowly decomposing from exposure to the never-ending psychological warfare and terrorism of a corrupt life behind bars. To eliminate crime, we cannot only rely on punishment as a deterrent. Otherwise, we may as well convert every school building and art centre into a prison. Or even better, we may as well allocate another R52 billion to buy more arms.

Conclusion

As you travel the journey in this book, it might seem as if you are reading a litany of horrors committed against women. This is because this book is meant to examine Zuma's rape trial beyond the narrow confines of South Africa and within the context of a global war against women.

One limitation of the book, however, is its exclusive focus on heterosexual masculine culture as if it is the norm and everything else is an aberration of nature. The focus on heterosexual masculinity is not intended to exclude other ways in which men may choose to express their sexuality and masculinity. Rather, it is meant to confront some of the negative heterosexual expressions of masculinity that arose out of the Zuma rape trial.

Closely related is the exclusive emphasis on women as rape victims. This does not in any way ignore the grim reality of boys and men who are expected to 'take it like a man' and suffer the trauma of rape and sexual assault in silence. We know from the reported Roman Catholic sex abuse cases, the sex scandal in Abu Ghraib prison in Iraq, horrific gang rapes in our own prisons as well as other unreported accounts of male rape, that men and boys have suffered deep psychological trauma. More research and documentation is needed to bring men's sexual wounds out in the open to heal.

Notwithstanding the above, the focus on women as victims in this book is intentional and inspired by the courage and tenacity of a remarkable young woman who, in spite of her fear, took a principled decision to fight a war knowing that she might not win. While experiencing anguish, pain, isolation, fear, self-doubt and many other emotions that we will never know or understand, she was strong enough to speak out against one of the most popular political leaders in South Africa. Like a child from a broken family, she was caught in the crossfire of the succession debate. Like a warrior, she refused to be silenced and amplified the muffled screams of many other women who have been raped by those who still parade their power (or lack of it) in the corridors of government, business and traditional and religious institutions.

It is clear from Jacob Zuma's rape trial that in the 21st century a woman who decides to lay a charge of rape still has to face insurmountable challenges. If she takes a shower, she is told she destroyed essential evidence. If she doesn't, she is not a typical victim and may be accused of lying. If she is raped by a soccer star, a business tycoon, a politician or religious leader, she should not bathe, hoping and praying that by some divine miracle male power will be sexually transmitted.

It is also clear from the reportage on the trial that a female rape victim who doesn't fight back is perceived as a willing participant. If she fights back, however, she runs the risk of injury or death. If she chooses not to speak out, she will die inside. If she speaks out, she is a devil and deserves to burn in hell. Either way there is a possibility of death. Therefore, it is better to speak out and, like Biko, die for an ideal that will live on.

It is for this reason that I dedicate this book to a daughter of the soil born to a man who dedicated his life to fighting for the return of Azania to its children. Many lives later, including his own, his child is forced to return to exile. What, then, is the meaning of freedom?

War against
women

'We all expected the world to be different than
it is, didn't we? Some of us believed in art, or
literature, or music, or religion, or revolution,
or in children, or in the redeeming potential
of eroticism or affection. No matter what we
knew of hatred, we all believed in friendship
or love. Not one of us could have imagined
or would have believed the simple facts as we
have come to know them: the rapacity of male
greed for dominance; the malignancy of male
supremacy; the virulent contempt for women
that is the very foundation of the culture in
which we live.'[1]

While contemporary world culture condemns the exploitation and denigration of others on the basis of race, class and religion, it appears that the only group that is still exploited and discriminated against is the female sex. Statistics from around the world demonstrate that being female is not only oppressive but can be life-threatening.

From conception to death, humans who are born female are threatened or subjected to forms of discrimination such as sex-selective abortion to prevent them from being born. If they are born, they run the risk of being killed. If they survive infancy and reach puberty, they have to contend with physical and sexual abuse by family and strangers, forced marriages, genital mutilation, sex trafficking and prostitution.

Throughout infancy, puberty and adulthood girls and women remain in the cultural and legal custody of their fathers, a responsibility that is later transferred to their husbands. Once they reach adulthood, they are faced with unequal access to educational, political and economic opportunities, sexual harassment, marital rape, sexually transmitted diseases predisposing them to HIV, and possible death resulting from complications during pregnancy and childbirth. If they survive sex slavery and terrorism and reach old age, they are scorned for no longer being receptacles of men's sexual desires. If their husbands die first (a situation that is highly likely because women are imbued with a tougher life force necessary to survive in a 'man's world'), they may be accused of witchcraft or suffer abuse as widows. All these forms of violence reflect the position of women in society. The risk is being born female.[2]

Discrimination against girl children

In Africa, Asia and many other countries that share a strong preference for boys, sons are valued. Nowhere is this preference for boys better illustrated than in the Bible, which, in essence, is a story about men and their sons. Women, on the other hand, had to go to great lengths to make sure they gave birth to sons for their husbands.

In Genesis, two sisters, Leah and Rachel, fought to give their husband, Jacob, a troop of boys. Leah gave birth to four boys in succession but Rachel was not able to conceive and gave her maid, Bilhah, to Jacob to produce sons for him. Bilhah gave birth to two boys. Subsequently, Leah became jealous and also passed on her maid, Zilpah, to Jacob as a wife. Zilpah gave birth to two sons. After a while, Leah gave birth to two more sons. Leah, however, knew that Jacob loved Rachel more and said:

> *'God has endowed me with a good endowment; now my husband will dwell with me, because I have borne him six sons.'* [3]

Similarly, in Buchi Emecheta's *The Joys of Motherhood*, Nnu Ego marries but is sent home in disgrace because she fails to bear a child quickly enough. Afterwards, she is sent to marry a second husband whom she finds old and ugly. In the marriage, Nnu Ego suffers extreme poverty and the pressure to bear male children wears her down. She is particularly shamed when she gives birth to twin girls.

> *'The men make it look as if we must aspire for children or die. That's why when I lost my first son I wanted to die, because I failed to live up to the standard expected of me by the males in my life, my father and my husband – and now I have to include my sons. But who made the law that we should not hope in our daughters?'* [4]

The preference for boys is founded on the principle and belief that the man functions as the head of and provider for the family. Sons therefore represent economic security for their parents and extended families. While daughters help with domestic chores, their contribution is not valued due to its reproductive not productive nature. In many ways, money earned by their brothers is seen to be more important than raising children. Instead, girls are perceived as an economic liability.

It is thus not surprising that a World Health Organisation study found that wherever food is in short supply, girls are fed less, breastfed for a shorter time, and taken to doctors less often.[5]

UNICEF estimates that one million female babies die each year from malnutrition and abuse. In addition, some mothers are known to stop breastfeeding early in order to try to fall pregnant with a son.

Access to food and education is another important consideration. According to an FAO State of Food Insecurity report in 2005, more than 121 million school-age children worldwide remain out of school. Of these, two-thirds are girls and most of them live in rural areas where poverty and hunger are widespread.[6] According to United Nations Secretary General Kofi Annan, addressing the gender gap in education remains the greatest weapon in the war against poverty. In most of the developing world, therefore, addressing school attendance and completion rates for girls is essential to ensure that the United Nations' Millennium Development Goals target of eliminating this gender gap by 2015 becomes a reality.

Female infanticide

To be born into this world and be greeted with a sigh of disappointment is regrettable for any child, but for a girl it can be a death sentence. Female infanticide is the intentional abortion of a foetus or the murder of an infant because she is female. This phenomenon is ancient and is reported to have accounted for millions of gender-selective deaths throughout history. In Greece in 200 BC, for example, the murder of female infants was so common that among 6 000 families living in Delphi, no more than 1% had two daughters.[7] In modern society, countries such as China and India still have pregnant women undergoing amniocentesis to determine the gender of their children.

Amniocentesis was initially introduced as a medical test to check for birth defects during pregnancy. However, this test has been appropriated as a sex-selection device, with the result of a possible abortion if the foetus is revealed to be a girl. In a study of 10 000 abortions following gender tests by amniocentesis in

40

Bombay, India, it was revealed that 9 999 of the aborted foetuses were female. Similarly, an official survey in China revealed that 12% of all female foetuses were aborted or unaccounted for.[8]

Medical testing for sex selection, though officially outlawed, has become a booming business in countries that still uphold the practice. There is a saying in India, 'Better 500 rupees now than 5 000 rupees later', meaning it is cheaper to abort the female foetus now than pay an unaffordable dowry later.[9]

Dowry deaths

Dowry is the payment in cash or in kind by a bride's family to the prospective groom's family. Common in India, paying a dowry is a practice reported to have originated in upper-caste families as a wedding gift to the bride from her family. Over time, a dowry was given to assist with marriage expenses as well as to serve as insurance for the bride in case her parents-in-law mistreated her.[10] Unfortunately, the practice is being abused with grooms often demanding large sums of money, furniture, domestic animals and electronic appliances. When the dowry is not sufficient, the bride may be harassed or abused. This abuse can escalate to the point where the husband-to-be or his family burns the bride to death.

Though prohibited by law in 1961 and followed by an amendment to the Indian Penal Code in 1986, the extraction of a dowry from the bride's family prior to marriage still occurs. According to government figures, a total of 5 377 dowry deaths were reported in 1993, an increase of 12% from 1992.[11] Even though the number of dowry murders is reported to be on the increase, it remains difficult to determine the exact extent of this practice because these deaths are reported as accidents or suicides by the family.

While dowries are mainly given in Asian countries, bride wealth (*bogadi*, *lobola*) is characteristic of sub-Saharan Africa. This involves the groom or his family giving gifts to the bride's family. An animal (a cow, sheep or goat) is slaughtered as a symbol of blood bonding between the two families and their ancestors. In theory, both dowry and *bogadi* were given in the spirit of generosity and kinship. Their commercialisation has, however, not only undermined the practice but has also created a perfect environment for the abuse of wives, who are treated as commodities.

In a study conducted by the Tanzanian Media Women Association (TAMWA) in 2006, it was reported that the practice of bride price has become one of the factors contributing to sexual abuse and battery of women, and the denial of their right to own and inherit property and land.[12] The survey revealed that men who cannot afford a bride price end up living with women and having children out of wedlock. The study also found that some parents took bride price as a form of financial investment and demanded exorbitant amounts of cash or other items such as livestock, land, motor vehicles and property in exchange for their daughters. In some instances, men are known to claim their money back when marriages break down. All of these factors leave women and children vulnerable to poverty and its associated social ills.

Honour killings

Honour killings of women can be defined as acts of murder in which a woman is killed for actual or perceived immoral behaviour.[13] This so-called immoral behaviour may take the form of adultery, refusing to agree to an arranged marriage, demanding a divorce or 'allowing yourself' to be raped. In the Turkish province of Sanliurfa, one young woman is reported to have had her throat slit in the town square because a love ballad was dedicated to her over the radio.[14]

Even though many honour killings occur in Muslim countries, with Pakistan reported as one of the countries where such atrocities are most pervasive, it is important to note that in many of the affected countries these murders are not sanctioned by the Muslim religion or national law. In April 2000 head of the Pakistani military regime, General Musharraf, pledged that his government would take strong measures against honour killings. In his pledge, he denounced honour killings as murders that would be prosecuted as such.[15] While the General's pledge was welcome, many were sceptical and unsure whether his words would be followed by concrete action.

In Africa one of the most publicised cases of honour killing was that of Nigerian Amina Lawal, who was convicted of adultery in March 2002. This case was brought to the courts in terms of the Sharia Penal Code in Nigeria that saw Amina accused of having a child after she was divorced. In a classic practice that discriminates against women, the father of her child, who swore that he had not had sexual relations with her, was released while she was sentenced to death by stoning. Ms Lawal's case was taken up by a coalition of Nigerian and international non-governmental organisations that provided her with lawyers, safe houses, and medical and psychological care over her eighteen-month ordeal. In September 2003, Amina Lawal won her appeal and was acquitted in the state Sharia Court of Appeal.[16]

In some situations, honour killings are reported to increase during times of war and conflict. For example, a report tabled by the Kurdish Women Against Honour Killings group alleged that more than a hundred women were killed by their husbands, brothers, cousins and other family members in the 1990s. Reasons given for the killings include, among others, adultery, a woman refusing to marry against her will, or marrying a man of her choice. In one case a lawyer representing a teenage girl from the Abu Ghraib neighbourhood in Baghdad reported that the girl was arrested after running away from her family with her lover. After months of negotiations she was returned to her family who promised to ensure her safety. She was shot dead a month later by her teenage brother.[17]

Honour killings reflect deep-seated and long-standing patriarchal beliefs and traditions. In a bizarre duality, a woman is perceived as a fragile human being who needs protection, while on the other hand she is seen as a devil from which society should be protected. Patriarchal tradition casts a man as a woman's protector, and this protection means taking control of her life. If the man's protection is violated, he loses his honour. The phenomenon of men's honour is central to the violation of women's human rights in many countries. Clearly, the vulnerability of women to all forms of violence can only be reduced if such patriarchal mindsets are confronted.

Female genital mutilation (female circumcision)

Female genital mutilation, often referred to as 'female circumcision', involves cutting away all or part of a girl's external genitalia. It is estimated that the total number of women who have been subjected to this form of mutilation is between 100 and 130 million. Given current birth rates, this means that some two million girls are at risk of some form of mutilation each year.[18] Most of the girls and women subjected to female mutilation are reported to be living in 28 African countries, although some live in Asia. Increasingly, others are found in Europe, Australia, Canada, and the USA – primarily among immigrants from Africa and southwest Asia.

The practice consists of the following:
- Circumcision: this involves cutting off the prepuce or hood of the clitoris. This is the mildest form and affects a small proportion of women.
- Excision: this involves cutting off the clitoris and all or part of the labia minora (inner lips).
- Infibulation: this involves cutting off the labia minora, clitoris and at least the anterior two-thirds of the labia majora (outer lips). The two sides of the vulva are pinned together with sutures (stitches) or thorns, leaving a small opening for the passage of urine or menstrual blood.[19]

44

All of the above operations are performed without an anaesthetic. The girl is held down with her legs wide open. Instruments used include knives, razor blades, scissors or pieces of glass. After the operation, the girl's legs are bound together from hip to ankle and she is kept immobile for up to 40 days to allow for scar formation.

The immediate and long-term health consequences vary according to the type and severity of the operation. Immediate complications include severe pain and bleeding resulting in shock, urine retention and infection, which can result in death. Long-term complications include cysts and abscesses, urinary incontinence, painful sexual intercourse and difficulties in childbirth.[20] The woman must be cut open on her wedding night to make intercourse possible, and the scar must be split to enable childbirth. Babies born to infibulated mothers may die or suffer brain damage due to prolonged or obstructed labour. Custom demands that a woman is sewn up again after childbirth – this may be done many times, depending on the number of children she bears.

While the origin of this cruel form of mutilation lies in the male desire to control female sexuality, there are a host of other beliefs that sustain the practice. [21] Firstly, there is the belief that a clitoris is an aggressive organ that threatens the male organ or may endanger a baby during childbirth. More deeply rooted is the belief that both male and female sex organs exist within each person at birth. The clitoris supposedly represents a male organ in a young girl at birth, while the foreskin represents femininity in a boy. As a result, it is believed that both the clitoris and foreskin must be excised. Closely related to this is the belief that the focus of sexual desire in a woman, the clitoris, has to be removed to protect a woman from being oversexed, thus saving her from temptation and disgrace.

The above beliefs have been challenged by a Ghanaian women's rights activist, Efua Dorkenoo. While she notes that excision of the clitoris diminishes sensitivity, she asserts that the operation does not reduce a woman's sexual desire because sexual desire is psychological. She further argues that the use of this custom as a 'preservation of virginity and the prevention of immorality' should be understood within the context of a society where pre-marital sex and loss of virginity for a woman provoke severe sanctions and penalties.[22] For example, in some African countries, the operation enables the prospective mother-in-law to determine if the girl is a virgin or not. If she is found not to be a virgin, the husband-to-be has the right to reject her. In many instances, the dowry is returned and the woman's family is stigmatised.

In essence, the woman becomes 'damaged goods' irrespective of whether sex might have occurred as a result of incest, rape or any other form of coercion. In this instance, the woman is the bearer of the cross of morality while the man is allowed to sow his wild seeds as widely as his organ can reach while at the same time expecting to marry a woman whose body is regarded as 'pure'. The double standards in interpreting the morality of sex as it relates to women and men are at the centre of controlling female sexuality, a phenomenon that will be addressed in later chapters.

Beyond the psychosexual reasons, female circumcision is also practised for religious reasons, which are fuelled by the belief that circumcision is a requirement of the Islamic faith. However, a research report compiled by Graham and colleagues found no general consensus about the religious motives of the custom. The authors believe that some of the confusion may have arisen due to a general interpretation of male circumcision; a view that is supported by Dr Hassan M. Hathout of the Faculty of Medicine at Kuwait University, who asserts that it is incorrect to view female circumcision as an Islamic tradition.[23]

In her book *The Hidden Face of Eve: Women in the Arab World*, Nawal El-Saadawi states that the value placed on virginity and an intact hymen in patriarchal societies is the reason why practices such as female circumcision remain widespread. Behind circumcision, she argues, lies the belief that by removing parts of the girl's external genitalia, sexual desire is diminished. This therefore permits a female who has reached puberty to protect her virginity and therefore her honour and that of her family.[24]

This cruel mutilation of women's bodies arises from a stereotypical perception of women as the principal guardians of sexual morality and as, supposedly, possessing uncontrollable sexual urges. Female genital mutilation is deemed necessary to promote virginity, a phenomenon designed to enhance men's sexual pleasure, which, in one sense, is derived from the ownership, control and conquest of a woman's body.

The denial of reproductive rights: the tragedy of motherhood

The patriarchal control of women's reproduction along with the irony that childbearing and childrearing are not regarded as 'work' lies at the root of women's subjugation. It is known that governments and men's social groups will give women 'permission' to use contraception or abortion when male authorities feel that there is a need to control overpopulation or the number of girl children being born.

In other instances, men's social groups can deny access to that right when male authorities feel that the population must be increased for political reasons. To illustrate: after the 1976 riots in South Africa some of the male comrades in the townships are known to have prohibited women from visiting family planning clinics. Because many young black men died as a result of brutal violent attacks of the white regime, black women were asked to stop using contraceptives so that they could replace the fallen heroes. Some of these women are known to have been assaulted by their partners for using contraceptives,[25] while others had to produce evidence of family planning clinic attendance before they could be considered for employment in some factories.[26]

Fertility control in many parts of Africa, including South Africa, has been influenced by the colonial policy aimed at containing black population growth. In South Africa such interventions included, among others, a state-sponsored contraceptive research programme housed within the infamous chemical and biological weapons research programme at Roodeplaat Laboratories led by Dr Wouter Basson.[27] Being housed in a biological weapons research programme, contraception stopped being about women's reproductive choice and freedom and became a weapon of mass destruction. The aim of this programme was to contain the rate of black population growth because blacks were perceived to be reproducing too quickly.

Other methods of contraception included prescribing contraceptives for women without medical supervision as well as forcing women to use harmful injectables such as Depo Provera or to undergo sterilisation without informed consent. In her paper 'The Late Apartheid's Search for a Racially-specific Immunological Contraception', Julia Brown argues that by its nature contraception is a technology of control often used and abused to control women's, rather than men's, fertility.[28] It remains ironic that at the height of apartheid, black women's bodies were torn apart when they were used by opposing forces as machines either to replace fallen heroes or to control black population growth.

In addition to the racial motives, such practices emanate from an exploitation of women in the name of the good of the community, i.e. a notion that smaller families reduce poverty, without addressing structural inequalities within society. Closely related to this is the exploitation of the role of women as mothers as opposed to being individuals in their own right. In many cultures, including African culture, a woman's personal identity is tied to her role within the family.

When faced with difficult social and personal choices, such a woman is tacitly trained to obey the rules (covert or overt) by making a choice based on others' needs and aspirations over her own. On its own, the notion of self-sacrifice and selflessness is not a bad thing. However, it becomes problematic when it is used to prevent people from realising their dreams and living their lives to their full potential.

Colluding with colonial governments, patriarchal religions and imperialists, husbands in oppressed nations readily collaborated with the struggle to suppress women's sexuality and control their fertility. Desire for control and ownership is reflected in fighting for ownership of land and women's bodies. This has found its way into nationalist and post-colonial reproductive health policies. On the whole, access to contraception, sterilisation and abortion remains enmeshed in male-dominated arenas and is based largely on patriarchal interpretations of the dominant culture and religion. In many ways, the modern woman is pressured into compromising her reproductive health rights when confronted with the multiple agendas of the state, religion, tradition, pharmaceutical companies as well as the broader global economic world order.

There is no doubt that lack of reproductive health rights and comprehensive reproductive healthcare for women is the main reason why so many suffer and die. According to UNICEF, thousands of women die annually from complications arising from pregnancy and childbirth.[29] Some of these women die bleeding in a van, a bus or donkey cart as their relatives search in vain for quick access to the nearest point of help. Some die from attempting to abort their pregnancies on their own, inserting a sharp object into the uterus or taking drugs, herbs or chemicals in attempts to induce an abortion. Most survive, however, often enduring a lifetime of guilt and chronic medical problems. Those who end up with chronic pelvic infections accept painful sexual intercourse as their lot along with feelings of guilt that come from an inability to refuse a partner's demand for sex. Others do not survive; they die in pain and alone with deep feelings of shame arising from being born female.

For every woman who dies, many others are sentenced to lives of trauma (physical and psychological), infections and disabilities that go untreated and are not spoken about. Considering that some of the women will suffer the trauma of repeated pregnancies while trying to give birth to a son, the cumulative effects of such traumas on a mother's psyche cannot be described.

Sexually transmitted infections: the gender factor
Sexually transmitted infections (STIs) represent a deepening crisis in women's health. A study by the World Health Organisation found that women with STIs bear the brunt of complications and serious consequences related to STIs, with thousands of deaths and millions of illnesses reported among women worldwide.[30]

Even though sexually transmitted infections can be prevented, their spread is perpetuated by myths and traditional beliefs surrounding female sexuality. For example, in some parts of southern Africa, there is a belief that encourages men with sexually derived infections to have sex with virgins to cure themselves. This practice contributes to the spread of these diseases (including HIV) among adolescent girls.

In addition, there are other socio-political factors that entrench traditional practices or encourage the spread of the disease. In South Africa, for example, the phenomenon of the migrant labour system, which necessitates men living in hostels far away from their families, has created an environment that condones multiple sexual partners, which in turn entrenches the ideology perpetuated by proverbs such as *monna ke selepe o a adimiwa* (like an axe, a man can be borrowed to chop different pieces of wood). For a wife who has been repeatedly infected with an STI, complications such as infertility may prove to be devastating, often resulting in scorn, ridicule, abuse or abandonment by her spouse.

We have seen from the Zuma rape trial, and other reports of leaders caught with their pants down, that monogamous married women are at greater risk of contracting STIs because of their partners' behaviour. In many instances, using a condom is perceived to be the man's decision. Fear of rejection or violence may inhibit women from acknowledging symptoms that could lead to early detection and treatment of STIs. For some women, chronic vaginal discharge, pelvic pain and pain during intercourse may be regarded as a normal part of being a woman.

Trafficking of women and sex tourism

Tourism has its own history that affects women and men differently. Traditionally, being female meant remaining at home, while being a man was a passport to travel. A woman travelling alone without an acceptable male escort risks being blamed for any 'harm' that may befall her on her travels.

Sex tourism is made possible through a network of local and foreign companies from Europe, North America, Japan and Australia that encourage men to travel to Third World countries specifically to purchase the sexual services of local women.

Sex tourism is part of a global market of human trafficking that trades in, among others, babies for adoption, cheap labour and sex workers. Fuelled by corruption in home and host countries, the market is run by an illegal underground operation that moves people across borders without the necessary paperwork. Many of the women and children intended for use in the sex industry are lured out of their neighbourhoods or countries with the promise of good jobs. Many end up in brothels.

Recently in South Africa, 26 Thai women were arrested in Durban after the Organised Crime Unit swooped on a club in Durban and a brothel in Pinetown.[31] The women who were arrested insisted that while they were in Thailand they were told of better jobs in South Africa. Once they arrived, it was reported, their passports were confiscated and they were forced into prostitution.[32]

This situation is, according to Joan van Niekerk, director of Childline, common throughout the country.[33] In many instances, she reports, women and children from different countries with no knowledge of English are sold as sex slaves. They are powerless, with nowhere to go for help. Rebecca Russell, a social worker with Reducing Exploitative Child Labour, concurs. Women and children, she reports, are trafficked for sex work from neighbouring countries such as Mozambique, Swaziland and Zimbabwe as well as from other countries abroad.[34]

For sex tourism to succeed, women have to be economically desperate to enter into prostitution. This implies that men's capacity to control women's sense of security and self-worth is central to the evolution of tourism politics. On the other hand, men from affluent societies have to view young girls as sexually docile, and women of colour as exotic, available, exciting and more submissive than women in their home countries, for sex tourism to succeed.

A 2005 report on forced labour by the International Labour Organisation revealed that forced labour, including sexual exploitation, generates up to $31 billion with most of this money being spent in the industrialised world. In Bulgaria, for instance, forced sex workers can only charge an hourly rate of $20 while a sex worker in the United States and parts of Europe can generate up to $67 200 per year. Sex slavery is also reported to be ten times more lucrative than other forms of forced labour.[35]

The success of this industry also depends on agreements between governments in search of foreign investments. Encouraged by economic advisers, foreign banks and technical development 'experts', governments in developing countries label the reputed beauty and generosity of local women as 'natural resources' to compete in the international tourism market. Current feminist debate argues that the eradication of sex tourism needs to happen within the context of the struggle for political liberty, economic reform and a strong call for a demilitarised society.

However, it is worth noting that sex trafficking is not only limited to the tourism business. A recent report by Julie Bindel in the *Mail & Guardian* reveals a proliferation of brothels alongside the beer tents and burger bars during the 2006 Soccer World Cup in Germany.[36] In Berlin, for instance, a 3 000-m^2 mega-brothel partitioned into wooden 'performance boxes' and designed to take up to 650 customers at any one time was built next to the main World Cup venue. To provide the service, up to 40 000 women had to be imported from Africa, Asia, central and eastern Europe and other poor countries across the world. The Coalition Against Trafficking in Women is reported to have received calls from mothers in countries such as Brazil raising concern about their teenage daughters being offered all-expenses-paid trips to Germany under the guise of 'supporting their country'. In other cases women were kidnapped and smuggled across borders.

The reaction of the teams playing in the tournament varied.[37] The French coach, Raymond Domenech, and the President of the Swedish Football Association, Lars-Ake Lagrell, are reported to have been appalled by the link between sex industry and football. Similarly, the Swedish government's equality ombudsman went as far as suggesting the Swedish team withdraw from the tournament. In contrast, however, the English Football Association's spokesperson, Adrian Cooper, reacted by saying that it was not their concern whether fans visited brothels. By not denouncing the sex industry, the English Football Association essentially turned a blind eye to a practice that allowed women and girls from poor countries to be bought and sold for sexual slavery. Given the high prevalence of poverty amongst women as well as disturbing reports of child rape and sex trafficking, one can only wonder what the Soccer World Cup in 2010 will bring for girls and women in Africa.

Conclusion

It is beyond the scope of this chapter to address all forms of violence perpetrated against women and girls. Common forms such as domestic violence continue to exist behind a veil of silence resulting in the loss of women's lives at the hands of those who profess to love them. For every form of violence mentioned in this book, many others exist in diverse cultural and traditional contexts across the world.

By not including women's activism and forms of resistance, this chapter runs the risk of presenting women's life experiences as a mass of doom and apathy. This is not the case. Women have resisted violence and oppression in many different forums and have achieved victories in international development policies, national legislative reforms, the increased representation of women in decision-making structures and a proliferation of gender and women's studies in institutions of learning. The most important victory is the impact of grassroots women's activism without which international declarations and conventions are not possible. Many hard-won victories have been gained through decades of fighting, lobbying, marches, legislation and policy change. If they are not sustained through vigilance and clarity of purpose, as we saw in the Zuma rape trial, women's rights can easily be lost to the wind.

War on sexual terror: a woman's body as a site for battle

'Even tonight and I need to take a walk and clear
my head about this poem about why I can't
go out without changing my clothes my shoes
my body posture my gender identity my age
my status as a woman alone in the evening/
alone on the streets/alone not being the point/
the point being that I can't do what I want
to do with my own body because I am the wrong
sex the wrong age the wrong skin....
...who the hell set things up
like this
and in France they say if the guy penetrates
but does not ejaculate then he did not rape me
and if after stabbing him if after screams if
after begging the bastard and if even after smashing
a hammer to his head if even after that if he
and his buddies fuck me after that
then I consented and there was
no rape because finally you understand finally
they fucked me over because I was wrong I was
wrong again to be who I am

which is exactly like South Africa
penetrating into Namibia penetrating into
Angola and does that mean I mean how do you know if
Pretoria ejaculates what will the evidence look like' [1]

Imagine that the hand throwing a US pellet bomb stopped for a moment before discharging hundreds of fragments over a small town in Afghanistan to check if the children at the local school were safe. Even better, imagine racist South Africa invading Botswana, penetrating ANC camps with a cocked machine gun but seconds before ejaculating a spray of bullets stopping to ask the question: is it okay if I ejaculate into you?

The poem above entitled 'Poem about My Rights' by June Jordan was once popular amongst many of us who fought the war against gender violence during the period leading up to the first democratic elections in South Africa. For us, it was important that we did not narrowly define rape as the penetration of an individual woman's vagina, but expand the definition to include broader and systematic violence against people and nations across the world. Shell-shocked by the reports and images coming out of Jacob Zuma's rape trial, I revisited the poem after more than ten years only to find shocking parallels between some aspects of the trial and the socio-political turbulence in broader society.

In this instance, the consequences of one African elder's inability to think rationally in one of the most critical moments of his entire life are purported to be part of a political plot to stop him from being the next president of the country. It is ironic that as a human race we remain tragically transfixed by the notion of men ruling political, religious and economic empires yet remain unperturbed by their inability to resist a woman's body enticingly wrapped in a kanga or thong.

'How do you walk around barely clothed in the house
of a man imbued with feelings? Any man with a

functional penis would have reacted the way Zuma did.'[2]

According to Busisiwe Mzala, a woman who travelled all the way from Herschel in the Eastern Cape for the trial, the only thing we need to worry about is the erectile power of the penis and not the rational power of the mind. Is it any wonder that we are fascinated by men's power to control global empires while we remain unmoved by their inability to control their penile erections? Does this explain why we are living on edge expecting to be wiped out by erect weapons of mass destruction poised at the point of no return with no option but to ejaculate?

Military aggression and invasion, inter-tribal and religious conflicts and other conflicts generated by competition for power or resources have become a reality of modern life. These wars affect the lives of innumerable men, women and children. For women and girls, however, trauma and death come in many other forms. Many are targeted for rape and other forms of sexual abuse. In addition to being attacked by strangers, women are killed in their homes and communities.

Guns, women and roses

Millions of people all over the world are subjected to violence in public and private spheres every day, with guns being the most common weapon. From civil war in Mogadishu to taxi violence in Soweto, gangs in Los Angeles and Mitchell's Plain, guns have become common instruments of death. Fuelled by the current 'war on terror', the arms industry is booming. All this occurs within a climate of weak gun control, particularly in poor countries.

The amount of money spent on arms is said to total an average of US$22 billion a year for countries in Africa, Asia, the Middle East and Latin America. According to an Amnesty International report, this amount would place those same countries on track to meet their UN Millennium Development Goals for achieving universal primary education (approximately $10 billion per year) and for reducing infant and maternal mortality rates (estimated at costing approximately $12 billion a year).[3] Furthermore, Amnesty International reveals that permanent members of the UN Security Council (China, France, the Russian Federation, the UK and United States) benefit from this spending as they are the top five arms exporters in the world. Together these countries are responsible for the sale of 88% of conventional arms, with the United States dominating the industry by contributing almost half of all the world's exported weapons.[4]

Overall, it is estimated that there are nearly 650 million small arms in the world today, 60% of them in the hands of private individuals who are mostly men. Similarly, the vast majority of companies that manufacture, sell and buy arms are owned by men.[5] The question then arises: what does this mean for women's safety in a world that has no regard for women's lives?

Less than a month after the death of former Yugoslav president Slobodan Milosevic and on the same day that former Liberian president Charles Taylor appeared in court for his crimes against humanity during the civil war in Sierra Leone, we woke up to an image of a boy toting a toy gun marching amongst adult males at Jacob Zuma's trial. The sight of this boy shouting slogans evokes painful memories of child soldiers in Africa. In her book *Child Soldier*, China Keitetsi gives a harrowing account of a child's journey from family to bloody warfare. The story begins in Uganda in the seventies when she, then eight years old, was drafted into the National Resistance Army fighting to depose Milton Obote. She eventually fled to Johannesburg where she was forced to temporarily inhabit the Hillbrow underworld before relocating to Denmark.[6]

Keitetsi's story is one of many of Africa's children. According to the Coalition to Stop the Use of Child Soldiers, Africa has the highest number of child soldiers. In Peru, El Salvador, Nepal and Uganda, over 20% of child soldiers are girls.[7] Many of these girls are forced into sexual slavery. A Ugandan girl soldier reported:

> *'The rebel commander ordered the soldiers to come and choose among the girls to become their wives. We all lined up, and a man came to me and raped me over and over again. I had to remain with him every night for the two months I was in captivity.'* [8]

Reports from across Africa show how difficult it is to integrate child soldiers back into civilian life once they are freed. According to Madeleine Yila Bompoto, co-ordinator for Integrating Child Soldiers in Congo, over 5 000 children are involved in the family reunification project overseen by UNICEF and the Congolese Ministry of Social Affairs. Many of them are reported to have been orphaned as a result of the war. A similar project in Sudan involves taking children out of the army, enrolling them in schools or setting up camps for them. However, because of limited resources, many children end up fleeing overpopulated camps to live in forests or in the streets. Some return to the army.[9]

The sight of the gun-toting boy celebrating aggressive and violent expressions of manhood was also a reminder of the fact that South Africa is one of the countries in the world with high levels of firearm ownership (licensed and unlicensed). Research has shown that a woman's chance of being killed by her husband or boyfriend increases fivefold if he has access to a gun.[10]

The lethal nature and severity of injuries caused by guns in homes are dramatically demonstrated by gruesome reports of femicide in the media. One such report stands out:

> *'Elizabeth Mhlongo of South Africa was shot dead in her bedroom in 1999, along with her five-year-*

old daughter Tlaleng. Her husband Solomon, a legal gun owner, emptied a magazine of bullets into the two victims, stopped to reload and then continued firing until the gun jammed. Elizabeth was left sprawled at the side of the bed, her chest, head, thigh and hand peppered with bullets, while Tlaleng lay slumped sideways in a blood-spattered chair.' [11]

Not only are women at risk of being shot by their civilian partners, those married to law enforcement officers such as the police, military personnel and other security officials are at greater risk. Just a day after the image of the gun-toting boy appeared, Superintendent Mateane stationed at Kagiso Police Station stormed into his girlfriend's home and killed her and several other people, including two women, a one-year-old boy and four senior police officers. [12]

Described by the local mayor as a 'very nice gentleman', Superintendent Mateane was driven to murder by an uncontrollable fit of jealousy and rage sparked by feeling rejected by his girlfriend. Very often, men's obsession to own women as their possessions drives them to kill in the belief that 'if I can't have you, no-one will' or 'I don't mind going to jail for you'. If a man lives in a macho and violent society with easy access to guns, murder can never be too far from the mind of a 'nice gentleman'.

If there is one thing that has been constant during Jacob Zuma's rape trial, it is the images and language of gun warfare (*kuzoliwa*) reinforced by a periodic rendition of what seemed to be a court anthem, *Umshini wam*. As a freedom song, *Umshini wam* was an appropriate and powerful expression of defiance in the face of an enemy who opted to use violence and war to enforce its repressive policies. However, if the song is sung at a rape trial by one of the commanders who fought for freedom in a country governed by people with whom he fought the war, it sends an irresponsible message to a young democracy that is still struggling with issues of racial and gender reintegration, gun control and violent crime including atrocious incidents of sexual assault of women and children.

Singing the song at a rape trial raises questions about the association of a gun with a penis. This association is a product of the warrior culture that has been part of society for centuries. In a book titled *An Unpopular War,* author JH Thompson describes white South African men's experiences of national service through interviews with former members of the South African Defence Force. In one case, an interview reveals the fusion of a gun with a penis.

> *'They had this little saying when you got issued with your rifle: "This is my rifle" (shaking the rifle) – "this is my gun" (and they pointed at their crotch) – "this is for shooting" (shaking the rifle) – "and this is for fun" (pointing at their crotch again).'* [13]

In another book, *Fire in the Belly*, Sam Keen argues that in warrior culture, a men's penis and his weapon become fused. According to Keen, the penis first became a sword and then a gun and a warrior's demonstration of his power.[14] Keen states that the Hebrew word for penis and weapon is the same, *za'in*.

The association of a penis with a gun in relation to Jacob Zuma's rape trial was articulated by Njabulo Ndebele in an article that questioned Zuma's capacity for self-mastery, a trait Ndebele argues is vital for anyone aspiring to high office. Of critical importance, however, is the association made by Ndebele between the AK–47 and what he termed the 'invasive penis'. Ndebele argues that the *Umshini wam* song rekindles memories of women and girls who are raped in this country.[15]

When he challenged phallocentric notions of masculinity, Ndebele came under attack from some men for being a traitor to the male species. In his response to Ndebele, David Masondo, national chairman of the Young Communist League, labelled Ndebele's analysis as an insult not only to Zuma but to those who asked him to sing the song. How does this response differ from defending Eugene Terreblanche's recital of a poem that affirms *die volk* at a trial where he was accused of assaulting a black man, on the ground that some members of *die volk* asked him to recite the poem?

Masondo asserted that Ndebele's analysis vulgarised the song and took it out of the context of a smear campaign.[16] Never in his response did Masondo bother to analyse the song within the context of a rape trial taking place in a sexist culture in a society where extramarital sex for husbands is tolerated despite the epidemic prevalence of HIV/Aids. Rather than putting the song within the context of widespread violence in a society that is still divided along racial, class and gender lines, Masondo chose to limit his analysis to one case only, that of Jacob Zuma who, according to him, is a victim of a political conspiracy plot. In no way could Masondo, as a young black communist, envision an anti-rape movement that also calls for a critical and incisive review of capitalism and patriarchy in the new South Africa. After all, both are deadly for black men and women.

However, while it is true that a poor woman's situation is bound to that of her exploited male counterpart, it is important that we do not lose sight of the particular exploitation that women face on a daily basis. Under the current economic system, an average black male worker is condemned to a life of poverty. His wife, however, is condemned not only to a life of economic exploitation but is also faced with the systematic practice of gender oppression perpetrated by her exploited husband.

In his book *Women's Liberation and the African Struggle*, Thomas Sankara, the revolutionary President of Burkina Faso who was assassinated in the course of a counter-revolutionary military coup in 1987, argued that the existence of privilege for a man spells danger for the woman.

> *'The male uses the complex nature of these relations as an excuse to sow confusion among women. He takes advantage of all the shrewdness that class exploitation has to offer in order to maintain his domination over women. This is the same method used by men to dominate other men in other lands. The idea was established that certain men, by virtue of their family of origin and birth, or by divine right, were superior to others. This was the basis for the feudal system. Other men have managed to enslave whole peoples in this way. They used their origins, or arguments based on their skin color, as a supposedly scientific justification for dominating those who were unfortunate enough to have skin of a different color. This is what colonial domination and apartheid are based on.'* [17]

Sankara called on progressive men to pay close attention to women's situations because they push Africans to wage a sex war when what they need is a war against poverty and economic exploitation. The fact that the Congress of South African Trade Unions and the South African Communist Party are divided over Zuma's rape trial remains a serious matter for poor black women and men in South Africa.

Rape as a weapon of war
Historically, the extent and nature of violence against women in the context of militarisation were largely ignored as a result of women's exclusion from efforts to develop a global rule of law. For example, out of over 240 representatives to the Diplomatic Conference that adopted the Geneva Convention, only 13 were women.[18] This means that the impact of war, conflict and

militarisation on women was not adequately integrated into these meetings.

Over time, however, the work of women's organisations the world over ensured that violence against women and girls during war became recognised as a crime. This resulted in progressive legislation and policy such as the adoption of the Rome Statute for the creation of the International Criminal Court in 1998. Adoption of the statute underscored the gravity of rape and other forms of sexual violence against women during war. The move was followed by UN Security Council Resolution 1325 in 2000, which calls for full participation of women in all levels of decision-making before, during and in the aftermath of a conflict.

Recently, the first sentencing of soldiers in the Democratic Republic of Congo for crimes against humanity stemming from mass rape was reported. Seven officers received life sentences while five others were acquitted by the Military Garrison Court in Songo Mboyo in the northern DRC, where members of armed forces raped at least 119 women and girls in 2003. Many of the victims were younger than 18.[19] The court sent a strong message through these sentences that rape is considered a crime against humanity and its perpetrators may face life in prison.

While the sentencing is cause for celebration, the overall implementation of the resolution is still insufficient. The UN Special Rapporteur on violence against women attributes this lack of will to an increasing backlash against women's reproductive rights within the current state of global insecurity. For this and many other reasons, the world continues to witness widespread violence against women during times of conflict. There are many ways in which women are targeted during times of conflict:

1. Rape of women as ordinary citizens of a country

Even though women may suffer violence as ordinary civilians in countries ravaged by war, some of the atrocities are gender-specific. For instance, violent attacks may be directed at women as 'bearers and carriers' of the next generation. In order to fight the enemy, one has to attack their women. Instances of mutilation of women's genitalia have also been reported. In Sudan, for instance, women's genitalia were mutilated as part of the war and would sometimes be displayed as trophies of war.[20]

In one sense, war increases and licenses rampant disrespect and disregard for women's bodies and their lives. In Iraq, for instance, the lawlessness emanating from the overthrow of Saddam Hussein is reported to have increased threats and incidences of violence against women. In June 2003, in the first months after the overthrow, Iraqi officers reported that the number of rape cases was substantially higher than before the war.[21]

One of the most gruesome rapes that occurred in the Iraq conflict happened on 12 March 2005 in Mahmoudiyah, a village south of Baghdad. On that fateful day, a 14-year-old Iraqi girl is reported to have been gang-raped and murdered by six US soldiers aged between 19 and 24.[22] In his commentary about the incident, Charles Laurence wrote in *The Star* that the gang rape and murder of Abeer Kassem Hamza Al-Janabi, and the murders of her mother, father and six-year-old sibling, were at first written off as collateral casualties of war. However, he argues, their blood will forever stain the honour of the US military.

It is important to note that rape during war is perpetrated not only by foreign and domestic armies but by ordinary male civilians who take advantage of the lawlessness that prevails during conflict. Similarly, it is also important to note that factors contributing to violence against women in situations of conflict have their roots in pervasive discrimination against women during peacetime.

The question then arises: does an absence of war mean peace for women? Even during times of relative peace, women live in a society that has no regard for their rights, including their right to safety and security. Situations of conflict are therefore not necessarily the cause of violence against women. Rather, conflict situations aggravate gender-specific forms of violence by reinforcing sexist stereotyping and rigid gender role differentiation. They also create conditions of severe economic deprivation, which make civilians totally dependent on authorities for accommodation, food, safety and security. In a situation where political and civil rights are suspended as a result of war, a dependence on authorities for livelihood and safety can be exploited, a situation that renders women vulnerable to sexual violence.

2. Rape of women who are relatives of male political leaders, army officials or members of an opposing group

Rape of women during war first attracted significant attention during the early stages of the Yugoslavian war after the mass rape of Croatian and Bosnian women by Serb militias was reported in the mainstream media. A few years later the well-known Rwandan genocide with its rampant rape and mutilation of women's bodies became etched into our memories. We would expect that after such global awareness, the world would react strongly and differently to a recurrence of such atrocities. However, women in Darfur in Sudan and other regions affected by war still tell stories of rape and abuse during conflict.

Rape of women during war is not a new phenomenon. In my interview with traditional elders in Ga Phaahla in Sekhukhune, it was revealed that women, children and cattle were taken as booty by conquering armies. They were appropriated as possessions by men who fought on the victorious side. In addition to changing their names to those of their conquerors, women and girls also played the role of sexual slaves and 'wives'. This means that women were forced into sexual relations with strange men. The same happened during biblical times.

Similarly, women in other wars such as the Second World War were at the receiving end of despicable treatment from armies of opposing forces. Linda Grant wrote in The *Guardian* that Berlin women were brutally attacked by Russian troops at the end of the Second World War.[23] The attacks were recorded and published as diaries in the mid-1950s and these include descriptions of gang rapes by ordinary soldiers and commanders alike. Grant also writes about a sexually repressive post-war era in Germany in which husbands reasserted their authority over women, forcing the subject of mass rape underground.

In such an environment, Grant argues, the main aim of the oppressor is to instil fear in the home and in society. If the oppressed remain voiceless and fearful they will remain silent. Ironically, she argues, the Red Army that drunkenly raped hysterical and petrified women was the same army that liberated the Auschwitz death camps. In a sense, the face of the victim and oppressor become one and the same.

Closer to home, we have heard reports of the rape of women in Alexandra township, on the East Rand and in KwaZulu-Natal by members of the Inkatha Freedom Party and African National Congress. Many women still carry deep wounds of gang rapes, and some live with both HIV and bullets lodged in their bodies. From my experience of working with victims of sexual violence in Alexandra, I can recall numerous stories of women who were kidnapped and dragged into hostels of opposing camps to be raped.

Because of patriarchal beliefs about masculinity, women are viewed as objects that can be owned. As a result, it is accepted that men in opposing camps can attack what they perceive as another man's property. Such a deep-seated belief explains why men resort to violence, including murder, to protect their honour when it is perceived to have been violated by an attack on 'their woman'.

In addition to the deep sexual scars that many women in South Africa carry as a result of the struggle for liberation, we will never know how many children were born out of this sexual terrorism. The sexual wounds of the struggle for liberation are like an abscess, which contributes to the silent yet visible decomposition of our collective souls.

3. Rape of women as activists, mediators and negotiators

In their role as human rights advocates, many activists campaigning for women's rights in a situation of war can be threatened, kidnapped or killed. They are targeted because of their visible or vocal leadership in the community. A woman from Baghdad University working for Amnesty International described her own sexual abuse at one of the checkpoints in Iraq:

> *'He pointed a laser sight directly in the middle of my chest, then he pointed to his penis. He told me, "Come here, bitch, I'm going to fuck you.'* [24]

Women held as detainees in the custody of US-led forces reported cruel and degrading treatment that included sexual assault in places such as Abu Ghraib prison. Several women who spoke after their release reported beatings, threats of rape and sexual humiliation.[25] While the sexual humiliation of male prisoners in Abu Ghraib exploded into the public domain through global media reports, instances where male guards were found 'having sex' with female detainees were not as widely reported. These female detainees were raped; it was not consensual sex. Any report of 'a soldier having sex with a female prisoner' needs to be investigated further.

It is important to note also that sexual abuse of women prisoners does not only involve rape. Other forms of torture include pregnant women prisoners being given electric shocks, medical care being withheld leading to miscarriages, body searches and forced vaginal examinations, and objects being inserted into women's vaginas. The use of strip-searching by British prison officials in Irish jails was an attempt to degrade and humiliate women prisoners in Ireland. The following is a testimony about a female republican political prisoner being strip-searched. The report was given by a fellow prisoner at the Sinn Fein Women's Department conference in Belfast in 1991.

> *'On the wing with me in Maghaberry was a woman from Tyrone, Pauline Quinn. Pauline's brother was murdered at the beginning of the year. Pauline was in an emotional state as you can imagine. A few weeks after this her grandfather died and she was granted a compassionate visit with her family. She went over to have the visit in the legal box. When Pauline came off the visit she was told that she had to go to reception. On hearing this she thought she had clothes to sign for.*
>
> *On entering reception, Pauline was put into a lock-up, which is a small room with no handle on the inside of the door and a small window with bars on. Then two security screws came in and told her she was going to be strip-searched. Pauline was forcibly pulled out the room and held down by eight screws and had her clothes ripped and pulled off her... She had her period at the time and her sanitary protection was taken away to be inspected by the so-called medic, who is in fact a screw with a white coat. Pauline's vagina was opened and looked into. She was then turned over and her anus opened and looked into.'* [26]

Like the physical torture inflicted on political activists by repressive governments, sexual violence is used as a form of torture on female prisoners.

4. Rape of women in the military

In recent times the world has experienced a growing number of women entering into the military. This shift in women's participation is a result of factors such as changes in military technology, increasing labour force participation by women and changing attitudes to gender roles.

In South Africa the increasing participation of women in the military is in line with government's commitment to gender equality. The White Paper on Defence reaffirms the right of women to serve in all ranks and positions, including combat roles. The South African National Defence Force is one of the few in the world that accept the right of women to serve in combat.

There has been a mixed reaction to women's participation in combat. In her paper 'Feminism and Militarism', Prof. Jacklyn Cock argues that militarism is more than arms–bearing and the practice of war. It has been defined as a set of attitudes and social practices that regard war as a normal and desirable social activity.[27]

The role of women in militarisation can be analysed from two points of view: sexism and feminism. The former excludes women from war on the ground that they are physically inferior and therefore not suitable for fighting. According to this view, women are the weaker sex and must be protected.

In contrast, however, feminism is not united in its view of women and militarism. One feminist view stresses women's rights to achievement, power and opportunity, including the right to make war. They therefore deny any inherent link between women and peace. Furthermore, this view maintains that the exclusion of women from the military is not dissimilar to the exclusion of women from political and economic structures.

Another variant of feminism excludes women on the ground that their innate nurturing instincts are not suitable for fighting. According to this view, the culture in the military is based on male stereotypes that reward violence and aggression and devalue attributes traditionally associated with women.

Recently, Idan Halili, a 19-year-old Israeli woman was reported to have added to the feminist critique of the military by sending a letter to the Israeli army asking for exemption from compulsory military service based on her feminist rejection of the military.[28] Halili argues that military service is incompatible with feminist ideology on several levels:

- The military is a hierarchical male-favouring structure and positions of high office are typically awarded to military achievers. This, she argues, favours men who are conditioned in a violent society and who do not have to break their service to raise children.
- The military distorts gender roles. Halili challenged the notion that women enjoy gender equality in the military because both sexes are conscripted. By its nature, the military reveres the male fighter and belittles the lesser female role.
- The military is characterised by high levels of sexual harassment. Rape in the military was concealed in the past but recent research findings have confirmed that women serving in the military are vulnerable to sexual abuse, including rape.

It is beyond the scope of this book to enter into a debate about the inclusion or exclusion of women in the military. Rather, I intend to reveal an existing link between military culture and violence against women. In 2005, researchers for the Haifa Feminist Centre found that between 2000 and 2005, 47% of Israeli women murdered by their partners were killed by security guards, soldiers or police officers who carried licensed weapons.[29] Similarly, a 1996 study by the Pentagon found that between 1991 and 1995 more than 50 000 active duty members assaulted their spouses. Within a six-week period in 2002, four women were killed by their husbands who were members of the

US Special Forces. Three of the men had just returned from serving as special operations troops in Afghanistan.[30]

In another report, Amnesty International research in Colombia in 2004 found that in militarised communities, gender stereotyping is exacerbated, thus increasing the risk of violence against lesbians. In late 2002 in the city of Medellin, a 14-year-old girl was stripped naked in the street and a sign carrying a message 'I am a lesbian' was hung around her neck. According to witnesses, she was raped by three men and her body was found days later with her breasts cut off.[31]

5. Rape of women combatants in armed groups and revolutionary armies

Just as in the military, an increasing number of women and girls are reported to be fulfilling combat and support roles in armed groups all over the world. Except in cases where women and girls are drafted into armed forces by force, women's participation in the liberation of any country is imperative because ongoing subjugation of women affects the attainment of freedom for all.

Women's participation in the liberation struggle, however, needs to be part of a broader empowerment strategy that is committed to translating 'revolutionary declarations to revolutionary practice'.[32] When addressing the concluding session of the conference of the Women's Section of the ANC in Luanda in 1981, Oliver Tambo challenged women to take their rightful positions outside the kitchen among the fighting ranks of the movement. Tambo urged women to educate and help liberate men from their ancient views about women.

> *'On the other hand women in the ANC should stop behaving as if there was no place for them above the level of certain categories of involvement. They have a duty to liberate us men from antique concepts and attitudes about the place and role of women in society*

and in the developmental direction of our revolutionary struggle... The struggle to conquer oppression in our country is the weaker for the traditionalist, conservative and primitive restraints imposed on women by man-dominated structures within our movement, as also because of equally traditionalist attitudes of surrender and submission on the part of women.' [33]

It is under the leadership of men like Tambo that women fought alongside men for the liberation of South Africa. It was also during that time that countless women suffered abuse at the hands of their comrades. However, many women who fought alongside men remain silent about sexual violence and harassment in liberation armies.

In the absence of formal reports, incidents of rape in exile are explored in works of fiction. For example, the film *Flame* focuses on the role of women in the Zimbabwean liberation struggle or *Chimurenga*. Events in the film cover the period during the height of the struggle from about 1975 to 1994 – 15 years after independence. The film's director, Ingrid Sinclair, assembled stories from female participants over a seven-year period. In her research, Sinclair found that despite their willingness to discuss their contribution and the challenges they faced in the guerrilla forces, women were reluctant to discuss these matters on camera. For this reason, Sinclair decided to make a fiction film.

Similarly, accounts of rape during exile are mirrored in literary works of fiction such as Mtutuzeli Nyoka's *I Speak to the Silent*. In the story a young woman, Sindiswa Kondile, leaves her home in the Eastern Cape to escape the racist regime and dies after a botched abortion in Lesotho. While in exile, Sindiswa is repeatedly raped by Raymond Mbete, a man with impressive political credentials who is in charge of a refugee camp. The repeated sexual violations result in a number of pregnancies with all but one being terminated. She dies alone after an abortion in a hospital far away from her family and community.

After his death, Mr Mbete's wife, Zodwa, testifies about Sindiswa's death at the Truth and Reconciliation Commission. Haunted by a feeling of complicity because of her silence, Mrs Mbete gives the following testimony:

> *'About twenty years ago I had the good fortune of knowing a young girl by the name of Sindiswa Kondile. I met her soon after her arrival in exile and I took an immediate liking to her. Because she was young and alone I asked her to come and stay with us in our house.*
>
> *The very first night she was in our house ... in the middle of the night I was suddenly woken by a noise, a muffled scream, coming from the guest bedroom where Sindiswa was sleeping. I noticed that my husband was not in bed. I got up quietly to investigate... The door to Sindiswa's room was open. I could see into the room, and what I saw shocked and frightened me...*
>
> *My husband was naked and on top of the girl. He was thrusting himself violently into her, and he had his hand over her mouth to stop her from screaming. She was struggling furiously. I could see her terrified face as the moonlight fell upon it. I could hear her muffled cries as she tried in vain to let a scream out...*
>
> *I spoke to Sindiswa the next day ... the bed sheets had blood on them. I knew then that she had been a virgin until that night. It seemed terrible that her first sexual experience should be rape by a man whom she thought of as her protector.'* [34]

Zuma's rape trial revealed that by the time the complainant was 15, she had already been raped three times. Upon hearing her testimony, many other hidden wounds of rape in exile were re-opened. Women who had been secretly nursing their sexual wounds could relate to her experiences.

> 'I kept silent because we were made to understand, earlier on in our lives out there, that the struggle for liberation was bigger than individuals. So when I was violated by the soldiers who were part of this grand and righteous struggle, I said nothing. My father told me I was first and foremost a young soldier and I should never point a gun (not even a toy gun) at a comrade. Guns were only pointed at enemies.' [35]
>
> 'I thought of who he was in the ANC and what came to my mind was to protect my leader. In exile, we were isolated, the movement was your family; good and bad things happened. Abuse is among those things that will always haunt many women.' [36]

The complainant in the Zuma rape trial was raped repeatedly as a minor in a situation of war. As an adult, she returned to her home country and was ostracised because of her previous sexual history, labelled a woman of loose morals. Just like Eve, she was condemned by Zuma's supporters to eternal suffering. Carrying the cross outside the court building and relying on a Bible that contains many unholy and horrific accounts of rape, Zuma's supporters cast the complainant as a temptress deserving to be stoned to death.

Those who raped her and many other girls and women during the liberation war are not man enough to take responsibility for their actions or make a call for a national cleansing programme that rids women of the hidden shame and trauma that emanates from rape in exile. Instead, their focus remains on what the oppressors did rather than what they did to their own people.

The Truth and Reconciliation Commission failed in its endeavour to create a safe space for healing women's sexual wounds. Invariably, opening such wounds implicates many men who are now in positions of authority within government and civil society. Faced with the possibility of equating the atrocities of the white racist regime with those of their comrades, women who were subjected to sexual violence during the war of liberation chose to remain silent.

This situation is not unique to South Africa. In her book *Women, Race and Class*, Angela Davis describes how, during the civil rights movement in the United States, black men who were accused of rape by white women were lynched. As a result, black women defended their men in ways that included bearing the personal pain of black men's harassment in silence. In many countries fighting for freedom, links between national liberation and broader women's emancipation were severed by the urgency and pressure to achieve national liberation now, and women's liberation later. This pressure forces sexual violation of women during the struggle to remain underground even after liberation has been attained. However, deep-seated sexual wounds do not stay buried forever. In her article 'Rape is a Weapon of War', Karen Williams reports that it is only now that Korean women who were raped during the Korean War are telling their stories after noticing that their granddaughters were developing psychological disorders as a result of the legacy of trauma that runs in their families.[37] In South Africa, the untold stories of how black women's bodies became sites for battle when they were raped by black or white soldiers are the unfinished business of the liberation struggle.

In African spiritual healing, a woman serves as a bridge between the unborn, the living and the departed. If the bridge has broken down, how can we ever talk about cleansing ourselves of the negative cycle of trauma that is etched in our collective memories? In an attempt to do this, Freedom Park in Pretoria is being developed as a place of healing. A garden of remembrance is being built that will heal the past through interventions such as cleansing ceremonies and bringing back the spirits of those who fell in distant lands. The main question, however, remains: do women have any significant role to play in national cleansing ceremonies? If so, what role do they play? Is it possible to lay the spirits of the departed to rest without the active and visible participation of those who carried them in their wombs?

In research that I undertook with traditional elders and healers in 2003 as part of strategy-building for the Freedom Park project, those interviewed revealed that women are not only bearers of life.[38] They are, according to the elders, the ones who communicate with the spirits during rituals. According to Venda custom, a man's sister, *makhadzi*, is the one chosen to speak with the ancestors on behalf of his family or community. In Tswana, Pedi and Sotho cultures, *rakgadi* plays the same role.

This information was passed on to the spiritual and physical architects of Freedom Park. However, the questions still remain: why was the national cleansing ceremony held on 27 April 2004 not led by a woman? Why did we choose to ignore the instructions of the elders and healers that the President should ascend Salvokop Hill in the footsteps of an elder woman who could intercede with our ancestors on our behalf?

The Freedom Park Trust was established to honour blood spilled by those who died for the country. However, this honour is limited to blood spilled at the sharp end of a spear or the barrel of a gun. There is no mention, no thought or consideration for blood spilled by an invasive penis. How do we expect to heal our memories when girls continue to be initiated into womanhood through rape? How will they pass on their roles as custodians of communities to the next generation? How do we ever expect to heal if we only honour the masculine warrior energy?

Honouring the masculine without creating sacred spaces for its healing is a futile exercise. As it is, there are many warriors who, like Jacob Zuma, sacrificed their lives for the struggle and never had time for an education. Many are scattered in squatter camps and townships and live each day without a sense of purpose or source of income. Most of these men, unlike their heroes, have to walk bare-spirited while their country celebrates thousands of millionaires as fruits of the black economic empowerment strategy.

These men are our heroes: they have shed tears, blood and sweat to fertilise a soil in which the seeds of black economic empowerment could be sown. They deserve to be honoured. However, we know from our grandfathers who fought in the world wars that a medal has no value for an empty stomach. Equally so, we know from spiralling violence and crime that the price of the economic boom in a nation that has no soul is high.

In addressing the soldiers' plight, it is important that we focus on developing skills that will make these men employable. Equally important are skills to help them reacquaint themselves with a life of coexistence and interdependence with their families and the nation, irrespective of political affiliation.

Similarly, the healing agenda in the country must include a woman-led, woman-honouring and woman-healing perspective. Instead of honouring a woman's life-giving blood, the healing agenda is surging ahead in an erratic fast-forward mode with most rituals being led by men. Like a menstruating woman, the feminine principle of compassion is viewed with scorn and ridicule. It therefore comes as no surprise that after President Mbeki suggested that the next president should be a woman, men in locker rooms and pubs came up with endless jokes such as: 'We'll have a head of state who's active 28 days a month – on the other two she'll have PMS and be considered a risk to national security'.[39]

Sexist jokes are one way that men deal with the reality of an unstoppable wave of leadership that requires the integration of feminine values and spiritual principles. Integrating feminine values goes far beyond the battle for gender equality, which has been reduced to fighting for a quota of positions instead of a change in consciousness.

Of course, we may ultimately have a woman president. However, without the consciousness of a leadership that honours intuitive thinking as much as it honours rational thinking, collaboration and not only competition, independence and interdependence, we may not see an end to some of the ugly battles in contemporary leadership. In the end, both the masculine and feminine are necessary for a balance between women and men, poor and rich, being and doing, and the outer and inner worlds.

6. Rape by foreign armies and peacekeeping forces

The role of foreign military bases as a source of violence against women and children has been well hidden from the public. In the 1960s and '70s, the world was informed of the murder of Vietnamese civilians and the destruction of villages. However, we know far less about the mistreatment of Vietnamese women by US troops. This involved 'searching' Vietnamese women's vaginas with their penises, applying shock treatment to their bodies, including their nipples and genitalia, and gang rape.[40] By raping a woman (either singly or with 'buddies') and later murdering her, a soldier stood a chance of gaining so-called double veteran status.[41]

As recently as 1995, in Okinawa, Japan, a 12–year-old schoolgirl was gang-raped by three military men in September when the Fourth World Conference on Women was being held in Beijing. Okinawa has been an island of military bases since the Second World War. Seventy-five percent of the island is occupied by American military bases where over 20 000 active-duty military personnel are stationed under the Japan-US treaty.[42]

The Japanese women who participated in the conference came home to this shocking news. They started a nationwide campaign and undertook research to uncover the extent of violence in post-war military society. The result revealed a litany of rape and murder of women including extreme cases where one woman was raped by up to 30 soldiers.

Similarly, women from the nomadic Masai and Samburu tribes have recently come forward with reports of rape by English soldiers in northern Kenya. More than 50% of the allegations involve gang rape. These alleged rapes are reported to have occurred over a period of 30 years in the vicinity of Dol Dol, north of Nanyuki in Rift Valley Province, Archer's Post near Isiolo in the Eastern Province, and in Wamba in Cort Province.[43]

According to an agreement between the British and Kenyan governments, three infantry battalions carry out six-week training exercises in Kenya every year. Approximately 3 000 British soldiers spend about a week in each of the training camps around the country. As of 2003, more than 600 women have come forward to report alleged rapes. Most were injured at the time of the assault, some were virgins and others fell pregnant. Almost all the rapes took place during the day when women were carrying out essential household duties such as tilling the lands, taking care of livestock, or collecting water or firewood.[44]

These women still report feelings of shame and humiliation and some experienced a breakdown of their marriages. Those who fell pregnant as a result of the rape gave birth to children of mixed parentage, who are in turn ostracised and labelled *mzungu* by other children. In certain instances, boys also reported having been sodomised. This is only the tip of the iceberg. Many other horrific reports of gang rape and sexual assault have been reported against foreign international armies, including UN peacekeeping forces.

In its condemnation of the Zuma rape trial, the *Sunday Times* reported that the foreign press lambasted South Africa, arguing strongly that the trial had serious implications for the spread of HIV/Aids.[45] The *New York Times*'s editorial was reported to have taken aim at Zuma's irresponsible sexual behaviour. While we might agree with the sentiments expressed by the foreign media, when they are viewed against the backdrop of sexual torture committed by foreign armies against innocent women and children across the world, such statements become hollow and hypocritical.

When foreign media networks descend on Soweto or Upington to document horrific stories of babies and women being raped by unemployed, brow-beaten black men living off social grants, they should make an equal amount of noise about the gang rape of innocent women and girls by white men wearing helmets, carrying rifles and backpacks in armies based around the world.

It would be hypocritical to focus only on the despicable actions of international armies whilst turning a blind eye to the role that the South African National Defence Force plays as peacekeepers in Africa. In a scathing report, Karyn Maughan wrote in *The Star* about sex-mad SANDF troops implicated in sexual assault in Burundi and the DRC.[46] It is worth noting that while such atrocities are committed by soldiers of all races, those mentioned by name in the report are white. This is important because we do not want to buy into the myth of hyper-sexed black men who cannot control themselves. Misogynist violence and patriarchy know no colour, creed, or political or religious affiliation.

The sexual offences reported in *The Star*'s article include:[47]

- A high-ranking South African peacekeeper stationed in the DRC facing court-martial for allegedly sexually abusing a teenage male interpreter.
- An SA Air Force Flight Sergeant sentenced to an effective 10 years in jail for fatally shooting his two young children and attempting to kill his wife.
- Paternity claims against different peacekeepers stationed at Burundi.
- A rifleman accused of sexually assaulting and beating up two Kindu women in the DRC.

- Five SANDF cargo handlers found in a UN vehicle with two half-naked women.
- A corporal accused of touching a female officer in a sexually inappropriate manner.
- A corporal who allegedly sexually harassed three female contingent members.

Sexual assault perpetrated by the South African army in neighbouring countries is a reflection of the rampant sexist and rape culture of post-apartheid South Africa. Rather than helping to address the increasing prevalence of rape in society, the Zuma trial seems to have given men carte blanche to 'act like men' and 'put women in their rightful place'.

Notwithstanding the above, it is important to note that for years Africa has not only become a dumping ground for organic and cultural waste, it has also been used as a receptacle for immoral values and despicable behaviour, which would be strongly condemned in other countries. Gang rape is not only limited to jack-rolling in Soweto. There are other fatal and lethal forms of jack-rolling perpetrated by armies of 'civilised' nations whose governments are known for their loud but hollow pronouncements on the protection of democracy and human dignity.

All forms of violence against women and children in Africa must be strongly condemned. However, their reporting should not fuel the spiralling wave of Afro-pessimism, which seems to have concluded that nothing human and positive will ever come out of Africa. This means that people who report corruption, underdevelopment, poverty, HIV/Aids and war in Africa must do so in a context that shows that Africa's rescuers remain her exploiters.

It is rather ironic that countries condemning violence abroad resort to war to make a living. In his book *The New Rulers of the World*, John Pilger reports increasing American arms sales following wars, with some of the most significant increases reported after the 9/11 attacks.[48] Pilger notes that the day the stock markets opened after the attack, military contractors immediately showed an increase in value. They included Lockheed Martin, a company whose main plant is based in Texas and which in 1999 recorded arms sales of more than $25 billion, and which had received more than $12 billion in Pentagon contracts.[49] Within six weeks of the 9/11 attacks, Lockheed Martin was reported to have secured the biggest military order in history: a $200 billion contract to develop a fighter jet.[50]

Likewise, Pilger reports a boom for the British military industry after September 11. For example, BAE Systems was reported to have sold a $40 million air defence system to Tanzania, a country with a per capita income of just $250 a year, where half the population has no running water and one in four children die before their fourth birthday. *The Guardian* reported on 30 June 2003 that BAE Systems had paid millions of pounds in secret commissions to obtain a huge contract to sell Hawk jets to South Africa. This landed South Africa in the arms deal mess, which, in my opinion, has cost the country an incalculable amount in economic and moral losses.

Given the above, why would leaders preach peace and reconstruction of a society when it is so profitable to make war? The governments of Western countries support arms manufacturers whose products are used in wars, which result in the rape of women and children, which then spreads HIV/Aids in an environment of gross poverty and social inequalities. Faced with the incalculable cost of HIV/Aids, poor countries ravaged by war and hunger remain at the mercy of rich governments who, like knights in shining armour, offload shipments of food, money and technical aid. With a little help from multinational pharmaceutical companies, rich countries rescue poor countries not only from hunger, but also from the debilitating effect of HIV/Aids.

Lucifer, deliver us from evil

'Husbands love your wives,
just as Christ loved the Church
and gave himself as a radiant church,
without stain or wrinkle or any other blemish,
but holy and blameless.
In this same way, husbands ought to
 love their own wives as their own bodies.
He who loves his wife loves himself.
After all, no one ever hated his own body,
but he feeds and cares for it,
just as Christ does for the Church.'

Ephesians 5: 25–29 [1]

One strange but very interesting phenomenon about the human brain is its capacity to remember events and images selectively. In all natural and man-made catastrophes, different people remember specific images that will later come to symbolise the catastrophe itself. The catastrophe has the potential to create new opportunities depending on the individual's state of mind and the circumstances surrounding the event.

For instance, many South Africans who were not interested in or ignorant of details of the liberation struggle had never heard of Tokyo Sexwale before the death of Chris Hani. The image of a strong man openly crying for his dead comrade was plastered on television screens across the country despite this not being the way men and boys are socialised in a patriarchal society.

Similarly, for those less ignorant about key figures within the trade union movement, Mbhazima Shilowa is forever etched into their memories as he gave an Afro-tenor rendition of *Hamba Kahle Mkhonto*. Ever since that day, many link the song with his image.

In recent times we have been bombarded by various media images of Jacob Zuma and his loyal supporters. Before the trial, however, images of Zuma varied from his role in addressing KwaZulu-Natal violence, his contribution to peace in Burundi and the image of him dancing and singing on stage with the Leeuwkop prison choir at the Waterkloof military base at the launch of the Moral Regeneration Movement. An image that is less common, however, is him making incisive and critical comments about economic policies that discriminate against the poor.

In the current comedy of errors, Zuma is touted as the man for the poor. Why? Because he has experienced poverty at first hand and dragged himself up from the gutter. Fair enough. The capacity to succeed against all odds is commendable. However, if personal experience of any form of suffering was a guarantee of inner transformation, Africa would never have had so many dictators. After being subjected to the horrific physical and psychological trauma of colonisation, African leaders in post-independence states should strive to govern in a manner that ensures that all Africans are accorded the highest form of respect in their roles as architects of their own futures. One only has to look across the Limpopo River to witness how easy it is for a champion of people's liberty to become a champion of people's misery.

Although it is true that people who have overcome difficult circumstances may succeed in what they do, the real challenge comes with being able to let go of being the victim – including blaming others for obstacles they encounter later in life. Similarly, the fact that someone is a byproduct of the masses as opposed to being part of the intellectual elite does not in any way guarantee that such a person will be a good leader.

Back to the opportunities created by the Jacob Zuma fiasco. If there is an agency that has gained significant mileage and airtime from the events in Forest Town on 2 November 2005, it is the ANC Youth League (ANCYL). Unfazed by concurrent revelations of their corrupt dealings with late mining magnate Brett Kebble, the Youth League remained hell-bent on supporting Zuma, who is also facing revelations of a corrupt relationship with Schabir Shaik.

Determined to protect the Deputy President 'against vultures who want his head at any cost', [2] Fikile Mbalula made it clear that the Youth League was not only supporting Zuma but also defending the principle of a person being innocent until proven guilty. If we were to lose this principle, it is true that we would be doomed as a nation.

> 'We will continue to defend our revolution and our leaders relentlessly, where we believe they have been treated unfairly. We stand firmly behind the ANC Deputy President precisely because he is in the dock, and needs the support of his comrades in trying times. **It is an act we will repeat tomorrow and the day after should another senior ANC leader find him/herself in a similar position.**' [3]
> (author's emphasis)

Mbalula consistently calls for truth to prevail. Who are we to judge? The ANCYL's undivided loyalty in the face of massive criticism may be the result of good intentions rather than the possibility of a future political pay-off, as has been claimed. Given the age of the Youth League's members, they still have a long political journey ahead of them. They have plenty of time to demonstrate that their fight is not about individuals and personalities but is a fight for truth and justice as opposed to power for its own sake. After all, as Nietzsche argues, when power becomes an obsession, it can also become self-defeating.[4]

Shortly after his acquittal on the charge of rape, Zuma ascended the stage to thank the masses for their support in trying times. After thanking one and all, the people's hero went on to perform a kwaito-style rendition of *Umshini wam* on the steps of the Johannesburg High Court. Determined to capitalise on his moment of victory, the ANCYL followed their leader from one province to another, embarking on a road show aimed at demonstrating the might of Zuma's popularity. This is an external power that belongs to the masses, and not to Zuma himself.

In many ways, external power is limited. It has to correspond with a person's ability to please and appease others. When someone is popular, they have been made popular by other people. This means that someone who is perceived to be powerful does not necessarily own that power; it belongs to the group. If the group decides to take their loyalties elsewhere, the person's power will vanish like morning dew on a hot day. To stay in power, therefore, people need to develop the art of operating from their egos, which boils down to appeasing, massaging and living your life according to the group's consciousness. Breaking away from the group's demands, expectations and prescriptions can cost a person their perceived power, something that many people do not have the courage to do.

To demonstrate their loyalty, the ANCYL organised a press conference immediately after Zuma's acquittal. In opening the conference ANCYL spokesman Zizi Kodwa said he would respect the court's ruling not to identify the complainant. He would, instead, refer to her as Lucifer, a statement that was reinforced by Mbalula when he said, 'She is very rich, we are told. This Lucifer is now living overseas.'[5] The ANCYL remained steadfastly focused on protecting their Deputy President against what Mbalula referred to as a public persecution reminiscent of an era when a person's guilt was determined by public perception and the penalty was being stoned to death in a public place.[6] This, however, does not apply to 'Lucifer', who, according to the Youth League and public opinion, is evil and deserves to burn in hell.

Referring to the rape complainant as Lucifer was bound to be received with disgust and shock by many organisations fighting against gender violence. However, such an utterance was a blessing in disguise. It gives us an opportunity to explore the true meaning of the name Lucifer and to illuminate the dark side of the Bible as far as women are concerned. Furthermore, an examination of women in the Bible creates an opportunity to open a well-kept yet emerging secret of rape within religious institutions.

Lucifer: what's in a name?
In any community, prophets come in all shapes and forms. When he referred to Zuma's accuser as Lucifer, Zizi Kodwa was, though unknowingly, playing the role of a prophet. He was calling for light to illuminate the valley of darkness.

The name Lucifer has always been understood to mean 'devil'. This identification is reported to have a long history in the church with its origins traced from a passage in the book of Isaiah (14:12) that reads:

> *'How art thou fallen from heaven, O Lucifer, son of the morning! How art thou cut down to the ground, which didst weaken the nations.'* [7]

According to Dennis Bratcher, in fourth–century Latin, Lucifer was the name for Venus, the morning star. It is composed of two words, 'lux' meaning light and 'ferre', which means to bring. So the word Lucifer essentially means bearer of light.[8] The misunderstanding is reported to have been a result of the mistranslation of original texts; some claim that the verse in Isaiah is not about a fallen angel but a fallen Babylonian king who persecuted the children of Israel during his lifetime.[9] The *Catholic Encyclopaedia* reveals that in Christian tradition, Lucifer is not the name of the devil but the state from which he has fallen.[10] Wikipedia.org confirms that Lucifer was originally a Latin word meaning 'light-bearer 'and that it was a Roman astrological term for Venus, the morning star. In astronomy, a morning star appears in the heavens just before dawn, heralding a new day.

By referring to Zuma's accuser as Lucifer, the ANCYL hit the nail on the head. She was indeed a bringer of light who was to help bring much-needed light following the period of darkness that gripped our country. The way I see it, our country will never be the same again. Once you have seen the light, you can never go back to darkness.

Light, however, tends to reveal our deeply buried secrets. It forces us to face our fears, addictions, greed and other negative emotions. There is no doubt that Zuma's rape trial presented a crisis for the nation. However, if it is reviewed critically a crisis has the potential to take us to a place of new discoveries. If we are willing, crises can teach us new lessons that take us beyond the point of confusion and stagnation.

In the case of the Zuma trial, one man was stripped naked in public. His private acts were embarrassingly brought out in the open not because he is more of a womaniser than other men. As an adulterer, he does not stand alone in a line of powerful and historical figures.

What happened to Zuma can happen to anyone. However, his deeds gave the nation an opportunity to look at its image reflected in his mirror. When such an opportunity arises, many are not ready to look at the image, let alone open their minds to the possibility of changing their values and perceptions of the world.

In this instance, the required shift must occur in perceptions about women, sex and power in a country with a Constitution that guarantees gender equality. This gender equality is supported by progressive legislation aimed at advancing women's empowerment and is reflected in the fact that women constitute 41% of the cabinet, 33% of the National Assembly, and include a female Deputy President, Speaker and Deputy Speaker.[11]

Sex and sexual abuse in the church
When discussing the link between sexual abuse and religion, I will only refer to Christianity and African traditional religion. From the outset, I would like to make it clear that my references are based on personal experiences and do not mean that other religions do not oppress women. All major religions – African traditional religion, Christianity, Judaism and Islam – are unjust to women in some way, yet still proclaim their respect for women. It is, however, beyond the scope of this book to detail the many ways in which various forms of patriarchal religion discriminate against women.

In his essay 'The Unfinished Business of the Liberation Struggle', Islamic theologian and scholar Dr Farid Esack argues that even though theology is said not to discriminate against women, its practice tells a different story. Quoting Dr Riffat Hassan, an orthodox feminist theologian, Esack argues that gender discrimination in religion is based on three theological assumptions:[12]

• Man is God's primary creation. Women are therefore not only secondary but are derivative of a man since they are created from his rib.
• Woman is blamed for the expulsion of man from the Garden of Eden, and as a result all of her descendants are treated with suspicion and contempt that borders on hate.

- Woman was not only created from man, she is also created for him. This means that her existence is only meaningful if it is measured in relation to that of a man.

There is no doubt that patriarchal religions have a negative impact on women's lives. Just as one of the steps towards the emancipation of women lies in providing a critique of the political, economic and socio-cultural sectors, we are compelled to do the same with religion. In their praise of womanhood, male religious leaders mainly focus their attention on women as bearers of children. As they shower praise on a woman as the custodian of life, religious leaders also remind her that a good woman is not only submissive and peaceful but also willing to sacrifice herself and her life for others.

Undoubtedly, the virtues of peace, non-violence, tolerance and selflessness are essential for harmonious co-existence, and they ought to be celebrated in all human beings. However, such virtues can also be used as tools of oppression for women who aspire towards leadership roles in academic, political, economic and other social institutions. For example, women constitute the main body of any religious institution yet very few serve in leadership positions.

In many ways, religious practice wields control over women's lives. Before we discuss sex in the church, let's answer some true or false questions.

- The church is a holy place.
- Sex provides nothing but pleasure for the body.
- A man who does not engage in sex will go crazy.
- A good woman cannot say no to her husband's sexual demands.
- All women are adulterers.
- All men are rapists.
- Women have power over men.
- Men have power over women.

- Men have uterus envy.
- Women have penis envy.

The questions above are but a tiny fraction of some of the peculiar sex messages that boys and girls and men and women are subjected to in our society. From Sunday school to pastoral Bible studies, initiation schools and music videos, women's magazines and military camps, pornography and kitchen tea parties, women and men are bombarded by messages that quell or ignite their fire in a misogynistic, erotophobic yet sexually obsessive society. Undoubtedly, organised religion has a big role to play in this regard.

The presence of sex and sexual abuse in the church and its link to religion in general were brought into the open, albeit indirectly, as Zuma's legal team produced witnesses associated with the church to prove that the accuser had a history of making false rape claims. In a matter of days, the witness stand was turned into a pulpit as pastors Sithembela Masoka, April Mbambo, Modianyeo Modise and Oupa Matlhabe[13] took the witness stand promising to tell nothing but the truth before God. They would know from Proverbs 12:17 that '*He who speaks truth declares righteousness, but a false witness, deceit.*' Because they are pastors, we assume that they understood the significance of their words and we can be forgiven (in case we have been fooled) for believing that they told the truth. After all, preaching, teaching and living truthfully and justly are at the core of their job descriptions.

One of the first pastors to appear as a witness was Pastor Oupa Matlhabe of Katlehong African Methodist Episcopal Church. Responding to the allegations brought by the complainant, he cast judgment on her state of mind alleging that she was sick and needed help. This man of the Lord said this without linking her alleged disease with an even bigger disease within the church, which involves sexual permissiveness and abuse.

A survey done in the Western Cape early in 2006, in which 1 306 youngsters were questioned by researchers from a local Aids project in collaboration with the University of Stellenbosch's theology department, found that churchgoing youth did not behave differently from their larger peer group.[14] Overall, the sexually active churchgoing youth were found to have a higher number of multiple partners. Sixty percent of the youngsters interviewed had not used any form of contraception during their first sexual encounter.[15]

It is clear from the above that the cardinal rule that prohibits sex before marriage has failed to effect significant behavioural change amongst young congregants. The phenomenon of multiple partners is, however, not only limited to adolescent sexuality but is common among married couples. It is clear, therefore, that the application of the holy commandment 'thou shalt not commit adultery' has also failed dismally and cannot be relied upon as an effective HIV prevention measure. I know from contact with religious women recovering from abuse that the disease in the church is not only related to 'consensual' sex practices amongst congregants but includes reports of rape and sexual abuse in the church, with a number of these rapes perpetrated by those in leadership positions.

The past few decades have revealed shocking media reports of rape by the clergy in countries such as the United States, Ireland, Australia, Chile, Argentina and South Africa. Investigations following the reports revealed a well-kept secret of how religious institutions have become a haven for dangerous wolves in sheep's clothing. Steven Tracy warns in his book *Mending the Soul* that abuse in the church is not a new phenomenon and is as old as humanity.

> *'Humans are no less sinfully depraved now than they were in the past. Abuse is rampant today, as it has been throughout human history – a point we must*

emphasize because few Christians, even Christian leaders, truly believe abuse is rampant through all segments of society and is even committed by Christian leaders.' [16]

Even though a significant amount of reporting on sexual abuse within religious institutions is focused on Christian churches, all patriarchal religions stand accused of oppressing and abusing women in one form or another:

'Man enjoys the great advantage of having a god endorse the code he writes. And since man exercises a sovereign authority over woman it is especially fortunate that this authority has been vested in him by the Supreme Being. For the Jews, Mohammedans and Christians among others, man is master by divine right; the fear of God will therefore repress any impulse towards revolt in the downtrodden female.' [17]

Even in churches founded and led by women, as is the case in some African independent churches, non-reporting does not mean that women congregants led by a woman who teaches respect for African womanhood are not subjected to various forms of oppression and abuse in their homes and in the church itself. I know this from personal experience – I am a member of such a church and am aware of accounts of non-reported abusive acts towards women.

The wound resulting from being raped by a priest or church elder goes deeper than the body and the mind. Abuse within religious institutions is, according to Steven Tracy, fed by rampant spiritual abuse that takes various forms including power posturing in which religious leaders are preoccupied with their authority and continually remind people of it, as well as performance preoccupation when spirituality becomes a matter of external performance rather than internal character.[18]

It is in such an environment that religious leaders can, according to Tracy, manipulate and destroy others in the name of God and the scriptures. Tracy argues that spiritual abuse creates deep-seated psychological and spiritual damage as well as deep confusion and perversion regarding the existence of God or the value of attending church. If the spiritual abuse also involves rape or any other form of sexual abuse by the priest, the wound goes deeper than body and mind – it cuts through the soul.

> *'It is to priests that they entrust their deepest and often darkest secrets. It is to the clergy that they turn for spiritual guidance, believing there is sanctity conferred by ordination, a belief firmly upheld by the clergy themselves. When men professing to be special representatives of God abuse this trust, it is a rape of the soul. For the victim it is as though God himself has abused that person.'* [19]

In the wake of reports of alleged sex crimes against women and children perpetrated by the clergy, some religious leaders and congregants saw these as an attack on the church. Like Miles Bhudhu carrying a placard 'Zuma raped' and parading in chains like Kunta Kinte at the rape trial, some of the members of the church adopted a siege mentality that sought to present the church as a victim. They refused to acknowledge that just like teachers, politicians, doctors, lawyers, business leaders, traditional healers and other men of social standing, priests can and do commit rape.

In certain instances, however, religious leaders called for the church to take full responsibility for its actions. In his article 'The SA Catholic Church under Fire', Günther Simmermacher, editor of the *Southern Cross* (the official journal of the SA Catholic Church), focused the attention where it belonged – on the victims of abuse.[20] He called on religious leaders and the church as a whole to acknowledge that some of its priests have committed deplorable crimes and that they, as a church, have a responsibility to believe, protect and reach out to the victims who have come forward to speak out despite their feelings of shame, guilt and fear.

Responding to reports of rape in the church, some international bodies also took action. The Anglican UN office co-sponsored a panel on The Vatican and Violence Against Women as part of the 47th Session of the Commission on the Status of Women on 12 March 2003 at the Church Center in New York. In her opening remarks, Sierra Sippel, a senior associate of Catholics for Free Choice, thanked the Roman Catholic Church, her spiritual home, for having been an outspoken critic of war, noting that Pope John Paul II had used his religious authority to persuade global citizens to make peace rather than war.[21] While Sippel charged the church for not being as vigilant and as vocal against gender violence, she acknowledged, however, some of the actions taken by church authorities in this regard:[22]

- In 1986, Pope Paul VI denounced forced sex within marriage.
- In 1989 in their pastoral reflection on conjugal violence, the Social Affairs Committee of the Assembly of Bishops of Quebec noted that some stereotypes used by the Pope were harmful to women. The bishops identified that gender violence stems from the stereotypes that subject women to male domination.
- In 1995, Pope John Paul II condemned violence against women in his letter to women.
- In 2000, the Southern African Bishops Conference published a commentary on violence against women titled 'Silent no longer: The Church's response to sexual violence'.
- In 2003, the US Bishops Conference issued a statement on domestic violence. In their letter they stated that violence against women outside and inside the home is never justified.

They also condemned the use of the Bible to support abusive behaviour in any form.

Despite the above, violence against women in the church continues unabated. Of all the victims of sexual violence, according to Sippel, the most vulnerable and least protected in the church are Catholic nuns. In March 2001, when the *National Catholic Reporter* released a story of the sexual abuse of nuns by the clergy in 23 countries, the church was silent.[23]

The tendency of male religious leaders to close rank and protect their own is not unique. It is a phenomenon used by those in power to silence the voice of the dispossessed and disempowered. Similarly, the spiralling of gender-based violence in the church and in society as a whole is tacitly condoned by men's silence. The conspiracy of silence is meant to keep such atrocious abuse out of the public eye.

Letters, denouncements and policies drafted to reduce violence against women will not have an impact because they occur within a context that condones the inferior status and negative perception of women in religion and in broader society. The letters are read and distributed within a culture that upholds the notion of men as the head of the home and as having authority over women. Such authority often results in control and oppression of women in all sectors of society. An example of this is condemning domestic violence and still expecting a woman to uphold her marriage as a sacrifice for her family.

'Unfortunately, when the Pope condemns violence against women, his condemnation is made vacuous by the patriarchal anthropology that he advocates. For after condemning violence in his Letter to Women, he then praises women who carry themselves in a submissive, obedient manner – a disposition that

enables domination and thus makes women vulnerable
to the exploitation the Pope condemns.' [24]

In a situation where divorce is prohibited, a religious woman married to an abusive man with no regard for women's lives might end up dead. Because she is expected to love, honour and obey, a religious woman may interpret the teachings of the church to mean that she has to tolerate a wretched life on Earth for an eternal life in Heaven. In this instance, caring for others ceases to be an admirable virtue but a foolish, self-destructive act.

> *'When my husband started beating me I went to report the matter to my priest. He said I could not leave because I have to think of the reputation of the Church. He also told me that I should carry the cross with honour just like our Lord Jesus. I went back home and the next thing I'm in hospital with a broken jaw.'* [25]

Similarly, condemning sexual violence against women in the church largely happens within a climate that believes that sex should only take place in marriage, as is written in the Bible. In cases where single women are mentioned in the Bible, they are often mentioned as virgins or immoral concubines, harlots and adulterers known to possess the power to derail a grown man from his mission in life.

> *'For the commandment is a lamp*
> *And the law a light*
> *Reproofs of instruction are the way of life*
> *To keep you from the evil woman*
> *From the flattering tongue of a seductress*
> *Do not lust after her beauty in your heart*
> *Nor let her allure you with her eyelids*

> *For by means of a harlot*
> *A man is reduced to a crust of bread*
> *And an adulteress will prey upon his precious life.'*[26]

Is there any verse in the Bible that can help to liberate men from the seductive clutch of a weak and wicked woman who, like a snake, is known to possess the power to 'reduce a strong man to a crust of bread'? Why so much focus and attention on a woman's power over men's actions? Is a man who has authority over a woman, as Christ is head of the church, incapable of making decisive sexual decisions? Is it possible for men to resist sexual temptation or the abuse of sexual power?

In a group discussion I had with young men in Alexandra Township a few years ago, one of the questions that came up in the discussion was: what would you do as a man if a woman professes love for you? Can you refuse her? Interestingly, the discussion became heated with talk about sex, not with talk about love. While one participant felt strongly about a man's rights to refuse a woman's advances if he is not interested, others were adamant that 'If *kuku e a itlisa* (if a woman offers sex) how can you say no? What kind of a man are you?'

Suffice it to say, societal perception of a woman's sexuality is, to a large extent, based on the interpretation of the story of Adam and Eve, which, in turn, is focused on the evil power of a woman as opposed to a man's ability to take responsibility for his actions. While the biblical premise that the serpent deceived the woman who in turn gave the fruit to the man remains true, a general interpretation of the story is intent on punishing the evil woman. This interpretation is upheld in spite of the fact that God not only punished Eve; Adam and the serpent also had to account for their roles in the Garden of Eden saga. Surely the Lord will not accept a lame excuse from a male leader who cannot control his lust for a woman's body or his greed for public money?

It is this view of a woman as the ultimate temptress that made it easy for Advocate Kemp J. Kemp, who represented Zuma at his rape trial, to find an army of African men socialised by a patriarchal religion to make moral pronouncements about women's tendencies to prey upon men's precious, God-given status or power. It was also not difficult for a court of law to collaborate with the church by delivering judgment on a woman's sexual conduct in this case.

Ironically it is in church and in court that the phrase 'My Lord' is used. Similarly, it is in the two houses of the Lord (the church) and Lords (courts of law) that human behaviour is judged. Isn't it also interesting that in two of the most patriarchal institutions in society, the church and courts of law, that men come to work dressed in velvet gowns, frills and lace without the risk of being labelled gay or transgender?

A number of the pastors called to give evidence at Zuma's trial were associated with the Wilberforce Theological College in Vereeniging, a college that is part of the African Methodist Episcopal Church (AMEC). The African Methodist Church was started by Richard Allen, a devout Methodist, who was born a slave in Philadelphia in 1760.[27] By the late 1700s, he had resolved to establish a black Methodist church that would address the needs and aspirations of those who were discriminated against and oppressed by the white community.[28]

In South Africa, no-one can talk about the AMEC without mentioning Charlotte Manye Maxeke, who travelled to America to join a choir and met Bishop Derrick of the AMEC, who arranged for her to study at Wilberforce University in Ohio.[29] While Maxeke was in America changes took place in South Africa. In 1892, the Methodist Church held a missionary conference in Pretoria. At the conference, black delegates were not allowed to attend the meetings of the white delegates, while the latter were free to attend meetings of black delegates. Furthermore, blacks were barred from holding any position on the board.[30] As a result, a Wesleyan preacher, Mangena Mokone, led a number of black delegates in holding their own meeting outside the hall, a move that was to be the beginning of the Ethiopian Church. In 1896, Mokone and Maxeke formed a unity that resulted in the birth of the African Methodist Episcopal Church.[31]

Later in her life, Charlotte Mannye married Marshall Maxeke, who held a BA from Wilberforce University. They both worked as missionaries in Pietersburg (now Polokwane) and later established the Wilberforce Institute for the AMEC at Evaton in the Transvaal as the province was called at the time. The influence of this dynamic woman, who was the first woman from South Africa to obtain a B.Sc., was felt far and wide. All her life, she fought for the freedom of black people and women. The revolutionary American scholar WEB DuBois had this to say about her:

> '*I have known Charlotte Manye Maxeke since 1894, when I went to Wilberforce University as a teacher. She was one of the three or four students from South Africa, and was the only woman... I regard Mrs Maxeke as a pioneer in one of the greatest human causes, working in extraordinarily difficult circumstances to lead a people, in the face of prejudice, not only against her race but against her sex... I think that what Mrs Maxeke has accomplished should encourage all men, especially those of African descent.*'[32]

Charlotte Maxeke died in 1939. Her ideas were progressive for the time. Long before gender equality became fashionable political rhetoric, she advocated the establishment of the Women's Section of the ANC and encouraged women to enter the political arena. Had she lived until 1956, Charlotte Maxeke would almost certainly have been amongst the women who marched to the Union Buildings in Pretoria in protest against the pass laws, and who demanded to meet with Prime Minister JG Strijdom.

We can deduce from the proceedings of the Zuma trial and from what religious leaders had to say about the complainant that even though churches may be founded on principles of equality and justice based on race and class, these principles do not seem to apply to women. At its core, theology has always been the domain of white men. Increasingly, however, black men have stood up against such biased theology, giving rise to liberation theology, which sought to link God and the day-to-day lives of black people. While the latter was to be celebrated, not all male black liberation theologians concerned themselves with the needs and aspirations of black women. The result of this omission was feminist theology.

Female theologians criticise the patriarchal and sexist ideology upon which Western Christianity is based. However, because women are not a homogeneous group and they experience oppression and exploitation differently, feminist theological reflections are therefore situated within a range of divisions such as Western feminism, black womanism, theology of the poor, African women's theology, etc.

According to Isabel Phiri, African women's theology belongs to the family of African liberation theology. In addition to challenging the colonial and missionary interpretations of African religion and culture, African women theologians endorse initiatives to integrate African culture with conventional theological reflections and practice. However, African women theologians warn that African culture, if treated as a static entity, has the power to oppress women.[33] Despite the divisions in feminist and women's theologies, challenging the sexist nature of mainstream Christian religion and the depiction of women in the Bible is an issue that is common to all.

103

Rape in the Bible

It is a well-known fact that some facets of religious teachings and beliefs have, over time, been used as agents of oppression. For instance, the notion of the early Israelites as God's chosen people was used as justification for conquering other people's cultures and land. Similarly, Christian history is peppered with stories of exploitation, war and subjugation of early European tribes and indigenous communities in Africa, Asia and Latin America. Missionaries used religious teachings to exploit and conquer others groups including black and brown people, poor people and women.

In her article 'Religion, Rape and War', Iris J. Stewart argues that when reading the Bible, the reader gets the impression that rape was part of everyday life and was perpetrated by warriors, gangs, fathers, kinsmen, kings and slaves.[34] The most common was the rape of virgins appropriated as booty following a war.

> *'And they warred against the Midianites, just as the Lord commanded Moses, and they killed all the males...*
>
> *And the children of Israel took the women of Midian captive, with their little ones, and took as spoil all their cattle, all their flocks, and all their goods.*
>
> *They also burned with fire all the cities where they dwelt, and all their forts.*
>
> *And they took all the spoil and all the booty – of man and beast.*
>
> *Then they brought the captive, the booty, and the spoils to Moses, to Eleazar the priest, and to the congregation of the children of Israel, to the camp in the plains of Moab by the Jordan, across from Jericho.*
>
> *And Moses, Eleazar the priest, and all the leaders of the congregation, went to meet them outside the camp.*

> *But Moses was angry with the officers of the army,
> with the captains over thousands and thousands over
> hundreds who had come from the battle.*
>
> *And Moses said to them: Have you kept all the
> women alive:*
>
> *Look these women caused the children of Israel,
> through the counsel of Balaam, to trespass against the
> Lord in the incident of Peor, and there was a plague
> among the congregation of the Lord.*
>
> *Now therefore kill every male among the little
> ones, and kill every woman who has known a man
> intimately.*
>
> *But keep alive for yourselves all the young girls
> who have not known a man intimately.'* [35]

In yet another story in Judges 21: 15–23, after killing most of the men and all the women of Benjamin, the Israelites became concerned with how to get more wives for the surviving men. To do this, they killed the men and all the women of Jabesh-Gilead who 'have known man intimately' and took with them 400 virgins whom they gave to the men of Benjamin. It transpired, however, that the 400 virgins were not enough and they had to come up with another plan. They then remembered an annual feast that took place in Shiloh, north of Bethel, south of Lebanon. The men were instructed to hide in the vineyards, waiting for the young women to come to the feast. Just as the young women came out to dance, they were kidnapped. If one considers the demographics of the time, how different are over 400 mass rapes in biblical times from the human rights abuses that occurred in Bosnia and Rwanda in recent times?

It is ironic that while the Bible and African culture control women's sexuality by prescribing virginity, it is virgins who suffer traumatic experiences. Is it any wonder that the loudest voices against abolishing virginity testing are the voices of traditional male elders? From the biblical passages referred to above it is clear that women who already knew a man were regarded as damaged goods while virgins were seen as pure and ripe, ready for consumption and conquest.

Currently in southern Africa, the worst threat facing young girls is the increasing prevalence of child rape fuelled by the myth that sex with a virgin will cure HIV/Aids. Before we label this a uniquely African phenomenon, we need to examine what has happened in other so-called civilised nations. In her paper 'Virgin Rape Myth', prepared for the Sex and Secrecy Conference in 2003, Charlene Smith reported that in Victorian England, brothels were stocked with mentally retarded 'virgins' because it was believed that a syphilitic man could be cured by having sex with a virgin.[36]

This obsession with virginity is a reflection of men's obsessive need to control women's sexuality, a factor that lies at the core of patriarchal sex. This obsession with controlling women's sexuality is reported to be the result of men's inability to determine whether their putative children are not their genetic offspring. For this reason, men introduced barbaric acts such as female genital mutilation, killing brides who do not bleed on first penetration, torturing and murdering wives who are suspected of adultery, and stoning women who have committed adultery.

In other instances in the Bible, women were used as bait to protect men against gang rape. In Genesis 19: 4–8, Lot of Sodom offered his virgin daughters to protect his men from being sodomised.

> *'Now before they lay down, the men of the city, the men of Sodom, both old and young, all the people from every quarter surrounded the house.*
>
> *And they called to Lot and said to him, "Where are the men who came to you tonight? Bring them out to us that we may know them carnally."*

So Lot went out to them through the doorway, shut the door behind him

And said, "Please, my brethren, do not do so wickedly!

"See now, I have two daughters who have not known a man; please let me bring them out to you, and you may do to them as you wish; only do nothing to these men, since this is the reason they have come under the shadow of my roof." [37]

In another incident in Judges 19: 24–25, a father protects himself from sexual abuse by offering his virgin daughter and concubine to a mob.

'Look here is my virgin daughter and the man's concubine; let me bring them out now. Humble them, and do with them as you please; but to this man do not do such a vile thing.

But the man would not heed him. So the man took his concubine and brought her out to them. And they knew her and abused her all night until morning; and when the day began to break, they let her go.

Then the woman came as the day was dawning, and fell down at the door of the man's house where the master was, till it was light.

When the master arose in the morning, and opened the door of the house and went out to go his way, there was his concubine, fallen at the door of the house with her hands on the threshold.

And he said to her, "Get up and let us be going." But there was no answer. So the man lifted her onto the donkey; and the man got up and went to his place.

When he entered his house he took a knife, laid hold of his concubine, and divided her into twelve pieces, limb by limb, and sent her throughout all the territory of Israel.'

Shocking as it may sound, the above passage could very well be from a modern tabloid newspaper, instead of from the Bible.

It is clear that rape is a message from one man to another. For a man who 'owns a woman', protecting his honour by means that may include rape and murder is particularly important. This is irrespective of whether such barbaric acts happen between blood relatives, king and servant, master and slave, men from different tribes, etc.

In many ways, rape is regarded not as a crime against a woman but as a violation of the honour of the man who 'owns' her. If the woman who is raped is married, the crime is more severe and may result in the murder of both the rapist and the woman. This is irrespective of whether sex was consensual or not. If the woman is unmarried, the man is expected to marry her or pay damages to her father. Such payment does not constitute a moral statement about the act of rape of one human by another. Rather, it is meant to compensate a man for the violation of his property.

It therefore comes as no surprise that Zuma would have been ready to marry the young woman he allegedly raped if he was required to do so. When responding to prosecutor C de Beer's question on how he could pay *lobola* for somebody he was not in love with, instead of responding that De Beer had no knowledge of Zulu custom and tradition,[38] he could have easily referred her to verses in the Bible that have rather striking similarities to what he called Zulu culture. Exodus 22: 16–17 reads:

'If a man entices a virgin who is not betrothed, and lies with her, he shall surely pay the bride-price for her to be his wife.

If her father utterly refuses to give her to him,

he shall pay money according to the bride-price of virgins.'

Similarly, Deuteronomy 22: 28–29 states:

'If a man finds a young woman who is a virgin, who is not betrothed, and he seizes her and lies with her, and they are found out,

Then the man who lay with her shall give to the young woman's father fifty shekels of silver, and she shall be his wife because he has humbled her; he shall not be permitted to divorce her all his days.'

In the case of Zuma, however, the woman was not a virgin. She had lost her virginity when she was raped whilst still very young and in exile. The men who raped her were not judged by the Bible but in terms of the rules of a patriarchal military institution. They therefore escaped being stoned to death. Further, the woman in Zuma's case did not only lose her virginity in exile, she also lost her father. This means that if negotiations about *lobola* were to take place, she would have no father to negotiate on her behalf. The one man who could have acted as her father-figure was the one in the dock defending himself against having raped her.

I find it interesting that what most people regard as African culture is also found in the Bible. This is indeed food for thought – especially for die-hard, self-appointed African traditionalists who speak about sexual morality on behalf of girls and women. Are we following the Bible or are we following African culture? Where does the one start and the other end? Can we cast the two aside and formulate a new human culture?

When we interpret culture and religion, we often tend to extract principles from the Bible and apply them to culture and vice versa. In my research study with rural elders on traditional measures of resolving conflict in the home, I found that many of the elders combined their interpretation of culture with that of the Bible. In some instances, teachings of African culture were either married to or combined with Scripture. Such a fusion is, according to African theologians, inevitable because of the legacy of colonisation and Christianity. There are close ties between the two and many colonised Africans are influenced by Christian theory and practice.

For example, an article on weddings and *lobola* by Isabel Phiri reveals that while *lobola* is a practice common in African culture, it was also practised in biblical times (Genesis 24: 53).[39] In their response to *lobola*, churches are reported to have taken varying positions that range from refusing to marry a couple if *lobola* has not been paid, to banning the practice because of its links to African traditional religion. In some instances, churches are reported to have taken a stand against the commercialisation of the practice, while others uphold the current trend of expensive weddings, clothes, a large church ceremony and reception.

In another article on the Bible and polygamy, Phiri reveals a number of polygamous relationships recorded in the Bible with the practice reported to have been widespread during the time of the Judges.[40] It was not uncommon for men like Gideon, David (who is reported to have married eight different women) or Solomon (who is reported to have married hundreds of wives of royal birth and kept many concubines) to marry many wives and father a great number of children. In her article Phiri notes that only sons and grandsons were considered worth mentioning in the Bible.

Phiri argues that the majority of African women theologians do not support polygamy because it dehumanises women. Polygamy, she argues, does not value a woman as a person but only as a bearer of children. Similarly, in her article on cultural issues in biblical messages, Eunice Okorocha argues that African culture is similar to Jewish culture in the value it places on male children. This means that in both cultures the birth of a male child is celebrated more than that of a female child.[41]

It is clear that modern religion, African or otherwise, disregards women's rights to dignity and remains preoccupied with controlling women's behaviour in both the public and private spheres.

Conclusion

I have always been aware of the negative role that religion has played in the discrimination and exploitation of women. I was, however, totally unprepared to find so many atrocious accounts of sexual molestation and femicide in the Bible. To deal with my state of shock, I went out to speak to a few of my associates who are staunch believers. While some were equally shocked, others had never read these passages. Others said they chose to read only the 'beautiful words' in the Bible. Where ignorance is bliss 'tis folly to be wise.

The situation is, however, not completely grim. There are initiatives such as the Bible reading practices at the Ujamaa Centre for development and research within the School of Religion and Theology at the University of KwaZulu-Natal, which uses Bible texts as tools for critique and transformation. By using the story of the brutal rape of Tamar that happened in the household of King David (2 Samuel 13), the Centre creates a forum for women and men to reflect on violence in their lives.[42]

While this calls for celebration, such efforts are few and far between. On the whole, Bible texts about rape or violence against women in general are not read on a Sunday nor are they used in group discussion for purposes of theological reflection. Factual historical data pertaining to slavery and oppression are often hidden from the oppressed to maintain the superiority of the dominant culture. The same is true of the religious conspiracy of silence on the violation of women's bodies.

To keep the majority of women in the dark about the impact of religion in their day-to-day lives, it is equally important to keep them submerged in gross poverty, overburdened by feelings of apathy and low self-esteem arising from unpaid reproductive and productive labour. In this way, all they do is find solace in prayer and they continue to fill up churches every Sunday listening to a male priest who may in his preaching, directly or indirectly, heap further scorn on concubines, harlots and adulterers. Certainly, it is not only in gangsta rap (as we will see in the next chapter) that women are portrayed negatively. The Holy Bible deserves its place in the hall of infamy.

Having said that, I feel it would be remiss not to ask the questions that continue to nag at me constantly: do we, as humans, have the capacity to evolve beyond our religious righteousness? Considering that many contemporary global wars are fuelled by religious differences, is it possible for us to transcend our respective narrow religious confines and communicate with one another using the universal language of love? Does religion differ from politics? Any attempt to respond to this question has to acknowledge the distinction between party politics and broader political activism as well as the distinction between organised religion and universal religious belief, thought and practice.

In his article 'What is the Church?', Samuel Ngewa reveals that the English word 'church' comes from the German word *Kirche* and the Scottish *kirk* with older roots in the Aramaic word *kenishta* and the Greek word *kuriakon*, both of which refer to 'belonging to the Lord'.[43] According to Ngewa, the church is both an organism (the dwelling of the Holy Spirit irrespective of where each member is located) and an organisation (a gathering of people around a common doctrine led by predominantly male officers acting as leaders of a group). It is my view that contemporary emphasis tends to be on the church as an organisation as opposed to the church as an organism.

For Africa, the trouble started when organisms were cut off from their daily prayers in shrines situated in caves, on mountain tops and near rivers and lakes. At that time, religion was a holistic approach to life that included dancing in a trance praying for rain and blessing seeds before the planting season, praying to thank the Earth goddess before harvest, praying to the Moon at a baby's naming ceremony, and saying special prayers and performing rituals for men before and upon their return from war. There was no such thing as Sunday mass. Mass could be held on any day, at any time, alone in silence or in a communal circle with other people.

Western religion brought with it a foreign education, language, culture and civilisation with the missionary at the forefront of a process of enlightenment. Explaining a direct link between religion and colonialism, Biko has this to say:

> *'A man who succeeds in making a group of people accept a foreign concept in which he is expert makes them perpetual students whose progress in a particular field can only be evaluated by him; the student must constantly turn to him for guidance and promotion. In being forced to accept the Anglo-Boer culture, the blacks have allowed themselves to be at the mercy of the white man and to have him as their eternal supervisor. Only he can tell us how good our performance is and instinctively each of us is at pains to please this powerful, all-knowing master.'* [44]

With the new religion, indigenous people's prayers changed fundamentally in form and content and they were told that prayers could only occur at a specific time and place. To become part of a collective, people were no longer required to take a hoe and join fellow humans in tilling the land giving life to a religious principle of *letsema* (similar to the concept of 'do unto others as you would like them do to you'), they were expected to join the church and carry membership cards as they would do for membership of political parties. Over time earthly aspirations for upward mobility permeated religious structures, resulting in power struggles within the church.

Politics is purported to be about justice and equality yet all we have experienced of politics so far is a bloody battle for external power. The same applies to religion. From my experience, religion (or is it the church?) does not seem to be the place to go to when one experiences a deeper longing for love and compassion. As a regular church-goer, I know and have experienced going to church feeling whole and returning feeling hollow. It is in such moments of spiritual emptiness that I ask: why do people go to church at all?

It is very clear that for some church-goers, regular attendance at church can occur without spiritual involvement. Similarly, many people experience spiritual enlightenment outside of organised religion. In essence, the divine does not reside in the church but in every breath that we take. Simply put, we are the embodiment of God.

> '*My spirituality is not set aside for special days such as Christmas, in special buildings called churches, synagogues or temples. My spirituality is every part of me. On some level I feel part of God/Goddess/All that is – not separate from it.*' [45]

This applies to all of God's creations. This means that God resides in all of us irrespective of our gender, race, class, political affiliation, popularity or educational credentials.

Finally, we know from history that Western religion treated African women as worthless and invisible. Despite oral and historical accounts of African women serving as priestesses and fulfilling a variety of functions including cleansing rituals as mediums and diviners and relaying messages from the Other world, Western religion treated African women as worthless and invisible.

African women also functioned as the main food suppliers, organisers and unifiers of family and society as well as the custodians of life. In his book *Song of Ocol*, Okot p'Bitek asks the question: woman of Africa, what are you not? From sweeper, smearing floors and walls with cow dung, cook, washer, planter, weeder and harvester, builder and storekeeper – all these (and more) were done to serve others and not for purposes of power and glory.[46]

If the church is to be relevant to African women's realities, it must first recognise these diverse activities and roles to be of significant theological or spiritual importance. Taking care of a child whose life is totally dependent on its minder is by far one of the highest forms of ministering. The church must confront all forms of discrimination against women within its walls and in broader society. A specific focus on all forms of violence perpetrated against those who are born female is, however, of critical importance.

In one such intervention, the Rev. Erica Murray of the Church of the Province of Southern Africa has put together a discussion course on sexual violence and abuse for use in parishes. The first lesson is about Susanna, who was threatened with rape by two elders who had been appointed as judges.

> 'Their moment came on a lovely hot day. Susanna went to bathe in her private garden and asked her maids to shut the gates and leave her alone. No-one was aware of the two judges lurking in the garden. Out they came, "We want to sleep with you. If you refuse, we'll testify against you." Susanna was grief-

stricken as she realized her dilemma. If she slept with them she would have to die (in terms of Jewish law of the time). If not, they would destroy her anyway. She refused them… She screamed, the judges screamed and everyone came running. The judges accused her of sleeping with a young man, which she denied. Because of their status, the judges were believed and Susanna condemned to death. Susanna cried out to God pleading innocence. God heard her plea and stirred Daniel's heart and he cried out loudly, "I want no part in the shedding of this innocent woman's blood." Daniel convinced them to return to court and to keep the two judges separate. This was a Jewish way of getting at the truth. One judge said he had found Susanna and the young man under a mastic tree, the other said it was an evergreen oak. All the people praised God for not failing Susanna. The judges were put to death and Susanna redeemed.' [47]

Capital punishment aside, ultimately truth prevailed. Susanna was not convicted for a crime that she did not commit. This principle of truth should apply to men who are convicted of a rape they did not commit, or acquitted for rape they did commit.

Burn the bitch

'Zuma for president, no matter what. This young girl is crazy and does not respect older people. She has insulted all women in this country, even those supporting her. She's a bitch and deserves to be jailed for dragging Zuma's name in the mud.'

Anna Mashele, cleaner at the bus factory, Newtown[1]

The word 'bitch' refers to a female dog. I have always been fascinated by the association between humans and dogs. In particular, I am intrigued by the sexual connotations of such an association. To satisfy my curiosity, I discussed this subject with men from all walks of life, all of whom are black. The choice of talking to black men was intentional because of my other fascination, the fact that relationship between humans and dogs in a country like South Africa is coloured by race and class. For example, a domestic worker who lives in Atteridgeville would never be seen taking her dog for a walk down the street in a local suburb of Tlhala Mpya. Yet, such an activity would be perfectly normal if she was taking her master's poodle for a stroll down Queen Wilhelmina Drive in Waterkloof, one of the leafy suburbs in the city of Tshwane.

I find the images of dogs buried in my psyche rather intriguing. The first that comes to mind is that of a 'kaffir'-

hating, red-eyed, pitch-black rottweiler baring its white teeth, barking aggressively behind a steel gate threatening to attack a group of pitch-black men, all pushing and shoving, trying to jump into the back of a white man's bakkie so he can take them to 'piece' jobs.

I'm never sure if it's piece or peace. Pieces of a dream – a dream of self-reliance, of not having to sit at a street corner waiting for economic salvation offered by a white man. Or is it peace? Peace – don't answer back, do as you are told, don't even think about arguing over your meagre day's pay. No sweat, *dankie baas*. Peace, as a young hip-hop rapper would say. *Le ka moso*, says an elder as he wobbles from a meeting at a local *kgotla* using his walking stick as a prop with his dog and loyal companion, Mantsho, limping behind him.

My story of dogs in South Africa would certainly be incomplete without the image of a German Shepherd. A German Shepherd, we used to say at Turfloop (University of the North), is trained to smell a darkie from miles away and to peel off the black skin of a student fighting for her right to equal education. Many a student activist has a story to tell about their bus being surrounded by boers and their dogs on their way to the funeral of a hero who was reported to have committed suicide in police custody.

I carry a vivid image of a hungry malnourished bitch that abandoned its puppies. As she ran across the road with her ribcage protruding from her chest, teats flapping from side to side, my mind immediately went to her puppies waiting for their mother to return.

The story of dogs in South Africa would not be complete without a mention of chauffeur-driven poodles transported to the salon for their regular grooming – shampoo, hair cut and ribbons. The image of a well-fed poodle clad in a colourful jumper with its groomed tail in the air can easily be replaced with that of an emaciated street dog with its tail between its legs surrounded by a mob of street kids carrying rocks screaming '*mgodoyi*' (starving dog), determined to stone it to its fateful end. I have often wondered whether the satisfaction that comes with taking a dog's innocent life serves as training ground for violence against human beings.

The story of black people and dogs is, however, not always grim. I grew up surrounded by dogs that had a sharp grasp of Setswana. I was raised by a mother who converses with cats and dogs as if they are human. She possesses an innate knowledge of and ability to communicate with other life forms, including animals and plants.

One thing I don't remember is my mother taking the dogs for a spin around Mabopane in her VW. When she did her errands buying veggies at the market in Boekenhout or her weekly ration of bones at Molewa butchery, she never took the dogs along. Instead, she always assured them that she would return to feed them as she reversed out of the driveway, and they welcomed her back with a characteristic high-pitched bark. It's true what they say; a dog is a wo/man's best friend.

Dog and bitch: the human and gendered dimensions

A few years ago whilst facilitating a workshop on gender and gender violence for a group of religious leaders at St Alban's Cathedral in Pretoria, I asked the participants to start with an exercise that required them to draw or imagine a symbol that best described who they were. One participant said he was like a piano. He said he possessed black and white keys. To produce a harmonious and melodious sound, he had to rely on collaboration between the black and white parts of the piano. This, he said, described his love for peace and racial integration.

Another priest said, to our amazement, that he was a dog. 'That's why I wear a collar,' he explained to our amusement. He went on to explain what kind of a dog he was: 'a watchdog for freedom, love and justice,' he said. For a moment, it was puzzling for us to hear a minister of religion describe himself as a dog. In our minds, the notion of a dog is associated with the most despicable and lowest form of behaviour. In daily township life, if someone calls you a dog, it is perceived to be the worst form of insult.

I asked a few men this question: what would you do if someone referred to you as a dog? One remarked first on the dog's loyalty, commenting that it is a trait that humans have lost. He jokingly alluded to the fact that it would be great to approach a beautiful sister on the street and ask: '*Sesi*, can I be your dog?' meaning a loyal and reliable friend. He went further to say, 'You kick a dog now, it wails in pain and a few minutes later, it is back at your feet.' I could relate to this last statement. In a decade of working with abused women, I have heard many a story of men kicking their (sometimes pregnant) wives and storming out of the house, kicking the dog on their way out.

Another man responded: 'Anyone who refers to me as a dog is looking for big trouble.' He saw the insult as the equivalent of someone spitting in his face. He associated being called a dog with utter contempt. It is this thinking that forces men who are called dogs to protect their honour.

Given the above, one would imagine that anyone stupid enough to refer to Nicky Oppenheimer, Patrice Motsepe or steel mogul Lakshmi Mittal as dogs would either end up with a broken jaw or a lawsuit on his hands. This was, however, not to be. A journalist who wrote an article in the Rich List supplement published by the *Sunday Times* on 6 August 2006 referred to these men as top dogs simply because they are 'the richest of the rich'.[2] With South African investments totalling R14,68 billion plus being ranked number eight in the world by the British *Sunday Times*, Mittal is a top dog followed by Oppenheimer, who is estimated by Forbes to be worth $4,6 billion, making him the 134th richest person in the world. Amongst them is a fast emerging dog, Motsepe, who, according to the Rich List, has moved from eighth to fourth place, increasing his wealth from

R2,85 billion in 2005 to R7,94 billion in 2006.[3] Lower down the list was Andile Ngcaba's Elephant Consortium that topped R6 billion in the wink of an eye. Only two women were mentioned in the Top 50 of the Rich List – Elisabeth Bradley and Philippa Johnson. If the men are top dogs, how does one refer to the women?

The discussion above is about financial power. It is, however, a phenomenon that can easily be transplanted from a board meeting to a street bash with DJs/MCs referring to one another as 'top dawgs'. A few years ago, my son wore a 'dog chain' as jewellery. Now that he is older, he has done away with being a dog – I hope. I asked him about the meaning of that chain and he responded: 'I was influenced by a rapper called DMX. He is a dog and I wanted to be like him.' Now that he has matured, he laughed at the idea. Our discussion made me wonder how many men and boys stay hung up on being a dog, a man, a bad nigga.

Other than aspiring for money and material goods, the dawgs don't only learn to spin the discs; they also perfect the art of spinning women. When you hear one man jokingly referring to another as a dog, *haai s'bali, u 'inja mfana*, chances are he was smart enough to avoid being cornered by two or three or more of 'his women' at a party the previous night. However, if the same two men were to fight over money, a woman or some other 'male possession' and one made the mistake of calling the other a dog, someone's blood might be spilled. Even more blood would be spilled if any of the top dawgs was to be referred to as 'bitch'.

The worst insult for a man who views himself as a top dog is implying that he looks or acts like a woman. In a training session a rugby player is constantly reminded not to attack like a woman but like someone who has 'balls'. The same principle applies to other male contact sports, careers and life in general. This means there is immense pressure on the man to 'represent', in other words he must go to extreme lengths, including using violence, to prove that he's got balls. This display of balls not only manifests between men fighting for a woman, it is a phenomenon witnessed within and between tribes, gangs, countries, religions and national and international economic conglomerates.

I know from my nursing training that human balls are not as tough as golf balls. They are made of delicate and intricate layers of tubes, nerves and blood vessels housed in an equally soft and tender sac. I also know that this sac (the scrotum) hangs outside of the body not to be an easy target to be kneed and kicked but because the process of spermatogenesis (making sperm) favours a temperature a degree or two lower than the core body temperature. Essentially, testicles have two primary functions – producing sperm and a hormone called testosterone. However, unlike women's ovaries, balls hang there for all to see – and kick. Since they are such soft and sensitive organs, I cannot work out why they should be turned into a symbol of masculine toughness, roughness and hardness.

Overall, men's constructions of masculine power are largely defined by who's up and who's down. As a result, real manhood is measured according to where it fits along the strong–weak continuum. Because the feeling that comes from being 'less of a man' is shameful and humiliating, it is critical that each man maintains his place along the continuum by means that may include coercion, force and aggression.

However, not all men are ashamed of being defined as being 'less of a man'. A few years ago, an interviewer remarked that Zakes Mda wrote like a woman. Mda regarded the comment as the highest form of compliment, which he felt meant that he wrote from the heart. Similarly, Nathan McCall talks about a need for men to be in touch with their humanity, explaining that people tend to confuse being in touch with their humanity as being feminine.

In his book *Makes Me Wanna Holler*,[4] McCall recounts the time while he was in prison when he was deeply touched by reading Richard Wright's *Native Son*. He identified with the character of Bigger Thomas whose racial fears led him to suffocate a white woman, which resulted in his being imprisoned. The book ends with Bigger waiting to go to the electric chair.

McCall recounts a passage when Bigger's lawyer spoke to him while Bigger waited to be executed. The lawyer speaks about how important it is for people to believe in themselves so that they can find a meaningful way to live. People's minds, the lawyer says, are riddled with negative messages that reinforce society's message of how bad they are, how useless they are and how bad their communities and people are. In describing his reaction to reading the passage, McCall said:

> *'After reading that, I sat up in my bunk, buried my face in my hands, and wept uncontrollably. I cried so much that I felt relieved. It was like I had been carrying those feelings and holding in my pain for years, keeping it pushed into the back of my mind somewhere... I was unaccustomed to dealing with such deep feelings.'*

For me, reading McCall's reaction opened my heart to two young men with whom I worked in Alexandra Township. I first met them in Leeuwkop and Johannesburg prisons while facilitating workshops on male violence. They were released from prison and participated in ongoing community education programmes. I still feel the sting of their tears when they faced the struggle of making a life outside of prison. I know that even today, they are still struggling not to resort to criminal activities that will see them being imprisoned again; a phenomenon that continually thwarts many black men's attempts to be fully human.

Fighting to be human in a world that would rather turn you into a beast is the most horrific life experience. Learning to 're-create yourself', as James Baldwin tells us to do, when we are overtly told (in the old South Africa) and covertly (in the new South Africa) that being black is bad is a painful but necessary long-term project.

'All you are ever told about being black is that it is a terrible, terrible thing to be. Now, in order to survive this, you have to dig down into yourself and re-create yourself... You have to impose, in fact – this may sound strange – you have to decide who you are, and force the world to deal with you, not with its idea of you.' [5]

Baldwin's and McCall's words apply to many black men I have met who had been ripped apart so badly by life that they felt they had to reclaim their power to feel. I have been deeply touched through my work and personal life by men's feelings about their ability or inability to feel. The ability to feel, as McCall puts it, is not gender specific. Ironically, Tupac Shakur also makes a point about men's ability to feel in his poem 'I Cry':

'Sometimes when I'm alone I cry, cause I am on my own. The tears I cry are bitter and warm. They flow with life but take no form, I cry because my heart is torn. I find it difficult to carry on. If I had an ear for confiding, I would cry among a treasured friend, but who do you know that stops that long, to help another carry on. The world moves fast and it would rather pass by. Then to stop and see what makes one cry, so painful and sad. And sometimes... I cry and no one cares about why.' [6]

When used by women to refer to a man, the label 'dog' is often a statement about the man's sexual behaviour. It is not uncommon for women who have had a negative experience with a male lover to refer to men as dogs. In this context it means that men are a lost cause and cannot control their sexual urges.

In addition to being a self-righteous stance on the part

of women, the belief that men will not and cannot change is based on a man-hating principle fuelled largely by rage. There are times when rage is the only appropriate response to the horrific forms of torture women and children are subjected to. Ultimately, however, a response that equates men with animals that are incapable of changing their behaviour lets them off the hook so that they do not have to take full responsibility for their behaviour.

The general principle of men being viewed as dogs is partly responsible for our tendency not to expect or insist on the highest form of moral responsibility and behaviour from them. This may be because we were never encouraged to expect moral excellence from men even though we look up to them as visionaries and outstanding leaders. Many of the lives of charismatic leaders the world over are tarnished by moral skeletons in their cupboards – a factor that in a 'normal' world would turn an intellectual giant into a moral dwarf.

Women as bitches and whores

The word 'bitch' is associated with weakness and a willingness to be dominated by a male dog. Nowhere is the notion of bitch used more abundantly than in hip-hop and rap music. For the purposes of this book, the terms hip-hop and rap will be used interchangeably. While this section will be largely based on US hip-hop, some limited references will be drawn from kwaito music – a South African version of rap music.

Even though rap music is said to have originated in the 1970s in the south Bronx in New York, many trace its origins to the '60s music of the Last Poets, Gil Scott-Heron and Millie Jackson, who were fuelled by the black pride theme in the speeches of Malcolm X and the Black Panthers. The fathers of artists such as Tupac and Kanye West are reported to have been Black Panthers.[7]

Jeff Chang traces the origins of hip-hop to what he terms

the politics of abandonment marked by municipal withdrawal and white flight from the Bronx, a situation that turned inner cities into places characterised by heightened racial segregation, poverty, community violence, drugs and gangs.[8]

Other cultural writers trace its origin even further to the enslavement of Africans across the world. This means that this type of music was born out of resistance and is a subversive vocalisation of the mistreatment of black people in society. From the era of slavery to the current Bush administration, people of African descent all over the world have been engaged in a struggle for life and death. Their music is but one of the weapons used to keep Africa alive in the face of European and American mental and economic enslavement.[9]

Even though the hip-hop and rap music industry is generally viewed as a male domain, women are reported to have been initially involved in the industry not only as performers but as entrepreneurs. Sylvia Robinson is said to have been a co-founder of Sugar Hill Records, one of the first commercially successful rap record labels.[10] The first rap song reported to have gone mainstream was 'Rappers Delight' by the male group Sugar Hill Gang released in September 1979, which remained on the American Billboard Chart for 12 weeks.[11]

Men's names are usually mentioned when people speak of DJs and MCs from the early days of rap music – Jamaican-born Kool DJ Herc who is considered 'the godfather of hip-hop', Afrika Bambaataa and Grandmaster Flash.[12] However, women such as Sha-Rock, MC Zulu Nation, Queen Lisa Lee and Spinderella, who performed with Salt-n-Pepa, are, according to Yvonne Bynoe, worth a mention.[13]

With the commercialisation of rap music in the '80s, hip-hop evolved into an industry that generated large sums of money for those involved in music video production, fashion, the club scene, television shows, video games, publishing and advertising. Beverage companies such as Coca-Cola have made a killing out of

126

the hip-hop world, a phenomenon referred by Ralph Ellison and quoted by Greg Tate in his article 'Hip-hop Turns 30: Whatcha Celebratin' For?' as 'the selling power of the black vernacular'.[14]

In his article 'Believe the Hype: Hip-hop and its Discontent', Kelefa Sanneh laments the fact that writing about rap is no longer writing about music but about 'capitalist wheeling and dealing' that involves money, drugs, women, clothing labels and record companies run largely by white executives.[15]

Many music critics argue that the commercialisation of rap music signalled the demise of social conscious groups. Darryl James wrote in *Rap Sheet* that most hardcore rap lyrics began selling millions once rap was discovered by young white teens looking for a rebellious tool to use against their parents. To them, it doesn't matter if the music disrespects black women or women in general. What they care about, wrote James, is being perceived as cool amongst their black friends as well as being repulsive to their parents.[16]

Greg Tate argues that such commercialisation not only changed the entertainment industry, it also changed people's notions of style and politics. This means that hip-hop encompasses the clothing label you wear, the company you keep, the car you drive as well as your attitude to political and other social issues, e.g. whether you vote or not. In South Africa a local TV advertisement targeted youth participation in local government elections using rap music and *scamto*.

In his critique, Tate makes a distinction between hip-hop as an art form and hip-hop as a cultural manufacturing industry. The latter, he argues, is approved in the boardroom and not on the streets, an assertion that is reinforced by Tricia Rose, who states that the genre caters to the lowest denominator and opts for racist and sexist content in order to expand market share.[17] Capitalist profits, she argues, don't have an investment in social revolution.

Given the multiple capitalist, imperialist and neo-colonial

agendas described above, one question remains: where do women feature? More specifically, where are black women located? How does racism and capitalism interact with patriarchy as this global drama unfolds?

Rap music originated as a way of challenging the status quo. This would explain why predominant themes include issues such as racist police brutality, economic hardship, drugs, alcohol and violence. However, since black women grew up in the same environment and were affected by the same conditions that the black male rappers rhyme about, why do they attack women? Why is the denigration of women a recurring thread in multi-lingual and multi-cultural rap music?

Male rappers are increasingly using violent and misogynist lyrics that depict woman as bitches who are expected to submit to being 'dogged' by men. This phenomenon is not a new one. From the rule of King Solomon to that of King Mswati, from the sounds of rock, reggae and folk songs deep in the African valleys, from Fela Kuti to Arthur Mafokate's dancers who gyrate while displaying their breasts and buttocks to a sexually addicted society, there is one phenomenon that has remained constant in a male-dominated culture – an absolute disrespect for women.

In some ways I think it is good that Mafokate (who continues to denigrate women covertly by means of lyrics such us '*Sika likhekhe*') is blessed with a daughter. It is only a matter of time before his investment in the plantation of patriarchy bears fruit when his own daughter confronts the deeply ingrained visceral pain of being a woman in a man's world.

Undoubtedly, it is clear that by employing shocking and graphic lyrics, young male rappers are following in the footsteps of those who came before them. Even though they may be condemned for 'unruly and disrespectful' behaviour that is perceived to be common amongst the youth of today, their actions do not exist in a vacuum but in a world whose existence and survival are at the mercy of rampant violence and widespread suppression of those who are powerless.

How else can we explain the motives of South African rapper Jub Jub, a boy fresh out of nappies with his trademark dummy in his mouth trying to sound like a man, rapping about shagging the hot girlfriends of less-endowed men?[18] At issue here, even for a boy of his age, is a pressure to demonstrate, by any means necessary, the mighty power of the male machine gun as he preys on those he perceives to be weaker than him. From black power to cock power, it's all part of the game.

'I just be conversatin' – an analysis of the lyrics and content of rap music

According to the artists, rap music is a vocal culture that demonstrates the power of the spoken word. If rap is verbal art, what is the dominant message and content of this art form?

A research study on the portrayal of violence against women in rap music done by Edward Armstrong between 1987 and 1993 in the United States provides some of the answers. In this study, Armstrong reviewed the work of thirteen artists presented in 490 songs.[19] He acknowledged that violence could be anything from an intimidating look, swear words, rape and murder, but limited his study to the analysis of three serious offences directed against women: assault, forcible rape and murder.

In the analysis, assaulting women was mentioned in 50% of the violent songs. The study uncovered intimate relationships riddled with violence, with most songs referring to women as bitches to be fucked and advocating violence in some way. Reasons for the assault include trying to end a pregnancy by kicking a woman (Ice Cube), handling a false accusation of paternity by trying to break a woman's neck (The Geto Boys) and injuring a woman and 'dropping her ass off at the hospital' (Too $hort). On the whole, the songs send a message that women should be hit, slapped and kicked for no apparent reason.

In this study Armstrong makes special mention of Eminem's

'Slim Shady LP' produced by Dr Dre, which won a Grammy in 1999. In the album, he reveals, women are killed by guns and knives and by innovative means such as poisoning. On Eminem's next album, 'The Marshall Mathers LP' (the fastest-selling rap album in the world), violent and misogynist lyrics are found in eleven of the album's fourteen songs, with nine out of eleven depicting killing women.

The study also reveals that songs about sex with a lover depict rough sex such as 'whip ass like a world champ' (Too $hort), or fucking a bitch so that she 'walks out of her crib with a limp' (Scarface) or 'breaking that thing in half' (Ice Cube). As far as rape is concerned, Armstrong found that rap songs advocated raping women who refuse to submit to sexual advances. There is also a mention of gang rapes where up to fourteen 'niggas' line up to take turns raping a woman who may be underage.

Discussing the results of his study, Armstrong warns against suggesting that all rap music is violent. Furthermore, Armstrong warns the reader against failing to interpret the violent nature of gangsta rap within the broader global culture of music.

Every form of music, he argues, from classical symphony to opera and rock reveals elements of male dominance over women. Punk rock, he asserts, is also a haven of 'male hegemony'.[20] This is echoed by Mark Anthony Neal, associate professor in black popular culture in the African and African-American Studies programme at Duke University. According to him, the art form expresses social ills, but it does not create them.

> *'Because hip hop is an easy whipping boy, there is a tendency to attribute the worst gender and sexual politics to castigate hip hop in lieu of having real conversations about domestic violence and other issues... We are critical of artists and of the channels, but are never really critical of corporate interests that are producing and distributing it.'* [21]

We could take this further and ask how we can become critical of ourselves and our children who consume this violent rap music.

Even though this study concerns itself with rap artists in the United States, many young people all over the world listen to American rap music or are exposed to it. In South Africa this has been actively encouraged by inviting a stream of American rappers such as Ja Rule, 50 Cent, Busta Rhymes, Snoop Dogg and Jay-Z to perform in our country. 50 Cent was hosted by the Johannesburg municipality, which was willing to fork out millions of taxpayers' money to pay one man to perform, spewing out profanities like a tennis ball machine. The money they paid to 50 Cent could have been used to revive and support a music education initiative like the Funda Centre in Soweto.

Foreign rap artists have often been reported to have smoked dagga on stage in a packed hall with teenagers. A US artist can afford to display this type of behaviour on a big screen in South Africa as they know that no action will be taken against them. But if South African musicians such as Stoan or Jah Seed tried to emulate this act in a packed stadium in America or Europe, they would be in trouble with the law. Many artists from Africa can tell stories of being arrested not for smoking on stage as the Americans do in our countries, but for merely being in possession of dagga.

Responding to the question whether rap music contributes to violence, Armstrong identified several research studies that show that gangsta rap motivates sexual aggression and inappropriate behaviour. This means that violent and misogynist lyrics contribute directly to the abuse of women.

In South Africa, while rhyming in local languages should be celebrated, if it used to convey violent messages towards women it merely teaches children to glamorise violence and misogyny. From the time kwaito hit the scene, musicians like Thebe sang about *kuku ke kuku*, followed by Arthur Mafokate's

Sika likhekhe and now the popular *Sister Bettina* by Mgarimbe. Running as a thread through many of these songs is reference to woman's genitalia – *kuku* or *khekhe* – as well as masculine power expressed in the form of sexual conquest aided by the male machine gun.

Even though the notion of male power expressed through sex is common in all cultures, for Africans the stereotype also plays to the clichéd image of black men's hyper-sexuality, a stereotype that was planted in human minds since the days of the trans-Atlantic slave trade. In his article 'What Do Men Stand to Gain from Gender Equality?', Faried Esack questions what he terms 'the lie of male superiority', which, he asserts, is a reflection of immense and negative gender conditioning that men carry with them.

> *'It's amazing that one's entire identity is located in a rather silly little thing that hangs between the legs. I find it both fascinating and absurd. What does this say about the rest of you, your values, your personality, and your identity if your strength and power is located in this organ? This is ludicrous. How can we allow the construction of masculinity to be so shallow and narrow? Why do we go round using a penis as a source of power and a weapon?'* [22]

In *Sika lekhekhe*, Mafokate asks the question: where are all the babes that desire me? His answer is: 'let them come and I will show them a miracle because I'm hot'.[23] In *Sister Bettina* Mgarimbe (real name Nkosinathi Mfeka) sings about horny bitches with open legs and men displaying the power of their balls by fucking women with impunity. In describing Mgarimbe's work, Ghetto Ruff website describes him as an artist who gives people what they want. His music, they assert, is music for the people. With tracks such as *Sister Bettina*, Mgarimbe is said to be destined for great things.

'Doggstyle': the depiction of women in music videos

Accompanying the graphic lyrics described above is the depiction of women as sex symbols, smiling seductively into the camera, wearing provocative clothing and dancing (usually surrounding a fully clothed man) with cameras zooming in on their bodies.

One of the most gruesome images mentioned is that of St Louis rapper Nelly, who appeared in a video swiping a credit card down a woman's backside. This led Spelman College in Atlanta to take action against the rapper, a move that was strengthened by *Essence* magazine, which started a campaign to combat the explosion of violent and hypersexual images of women in rap music.

Yet another image that stands out is the one on the cover of Snoop Dogg's album, *Doggstyle*, which shows an image of a naked black woman's buttocks sticking out of a doghouse complete with 'Beware of the dog' sign. bell hooks reports that the same image was 'uncritically' reproduced in *Time* magazine's issue of 29 November 1993.[24]

Reacting to the image, bell hooks wondered whether, if 'a naked white female body had been inside the doghouse, presumably waiting to be fucked from behind, *Time* would have reproduced an image of the cover along with their review'. hooks went on to say that when she sees the image that graces the cover of *Doggstyle* she not only thinks of young black men, but also of the sexist misogynist politics of the powerful white (and sometimes black) women and men who helped to produce and market the album.

hooks argues that a focus on the politics of the powerful should not silence black feminist critique under the guise of black women supporting their men.

'If black men are betraying us through acts of male violence, we save ourselves and the race by resisting.'[25]

Combined with the name-calling in the lyrics, music videos are meant to reinforce and prove that women are happy in their role of satiating male desire and lust. Music video production, like the music itself, is mainly overseen by men who have their own sexist notions of womanhood represented by a beautiful, sensuous woman ready to be seduced. The proliferation of such images in the media is a powerful way of ensuring that girls and women continue to believe this and remain enslaved to the hype. This is essential for ensuring a sustainable supply of women who are willing to do anything for attention, a drink and money.

Starting at a very young age, girls consume the lyrics and images in these videos and internalise the message that this is how women should act. At pre-school age, little girls have already mastered the art of moving their pelvises just as they do on television. Spurred on by an equally flourishing fashion industry and the page three hot babes, by the time they reach puberty these girls have dreams of making it in music or dance and appearing on television just like Lebo Mathosa or Thembi Seete. For these girls, being listed in *FHM*'s 100 Sexiest Women in the World is an ambition that is more accessible than a listing in *Forbes* magazine.

The fact that young people are the prime targets of advertising does not make it any easier for a girl whose future success is perceived to be tied to a man's bank balance. There is a proverb in Tswana, *Lore le ojwa le sa le metsi*, or in Zulu *libunjwa lisemanzi*, which means a rod can be bent without the risk of breaking when it is still wet or, in the latter proverb, clay must be moulded when it is wet because once it dries up, it cannot be changed. The proverbs mean that if you want to effect long-lasting change in a person, do so when they are still young and impressionable. Young people's impressionable state and the effects of peer pressure serve the market favourably. From technological gadgets to fashionable jeans, rap music and alcohol, young people are lured by the seductive messages and images portrayed by the mass media into the illusion that you have to have these material things in order to have arrived in the new South Africa.

A youth brand survey titled Generation Next undertaken by Monash South Africa in association with the *Sunday Times* on 30 July 2006 revealed that teens' top brands were Levi's, Adidas, Billabong, Coca-Cola, Nike, DSTV, BMW, Vodacom and Samsung (in order of preference).[26] With a flooded youth market, children call the shots in the consumer market years before they earn their first salary. In many ways they are thoroughly prepared for the grand lifestyle of a top player in the global market.

As is the case with pornography and tabloid newspapers, portrayal of women in music videos is based on the premise that sex sells. In her article 'The Exploitation of Women in Hip-hop Culture' Ayanna argues that pressure to use sex to survive can be traced to slavery, a phenomenon that resulted in a stereotypical image of a black woman as an oversexed individual, like her male counterpart.[27] During this era, Ayanna argues, women were under constant economic and psychological pressure to have sexual relations with slave masters and other slaves who desired them. In other cases, as illustrated in the chapter in this book entitled 'War against women', women were used as breeding machines to produce an adequate supply of replacements in the liberation of South Africa.

The phenomenon of women being forced to sell their bodies for their livelihood is common the world over. In a modern-day Africa that is ravaged by war and characterised by a spiralling number of women refugees who are dependent on warlords and male superiors for their safety, sex for survival is not out of the question. Similarly, an increasing number of women and girls living with HIV/Aids in a food-insecure Africa are forced to sell their bodies for food and money. This means that the depiction of women as gold diggers in rap music videos does not happen in isolation but in a society that still views a woman's livelihood to be dependent on a man's.

While the advancements made in South Africa with regard to women's access to business and professional life should be celebrated, we need a constant reminder that for every woman who makes it, many others still base their source of livelihood on what they can do for or get from a man. For young women like musician Kelly Khumalo, this includes posing half-naked as a 'virgin' and playing to the stereotype of an innocent woman available for consumption.

In an interview in *Y-Mag* Khumalo responds to Kabomo's questions with an attitude that says 'I am an It girl'. Behind this display of sexual confidence, however, is the voice of a little girl desperate for male approval, hoping to make it big.

> *'I don't seek attention, attention seeks me… I'm an entertainer, that's what I do, and that's why I attract attention to myself, and I do enjoy it when I get it. Even when I was a little girl, I used to love people looking at me.'* [28]

Khumalo uses culture and tradition when it suits the prescriptions of the dominant culture, and responds to the interviewer's question about how she feels about men's reactions to her sexuality by saying:

> *'I'm fine with it, actually it's not my issue, it's theirs,* ngiyi tjitsji, *I'm a young African woman, culturally,* amatjitji *should wear even more revealing clothes than the stuff I wear.'* [29]

136

Catching a top dog for one's livelihood is, however, not reserved for beautiful young things prowling the brightly lit streets of the big city scene. It is a phenomenon that is also witnessed amongst professional women in all sectors of society. Whilst not as overt as in the showbiz scene, calculating a woman's worth by her attachment to a man and her sexual attractiveness is common in all sectors of society.

Rather than condemn young women in isolation, their contradictions can be used as a barometer of the extent of the work that women still have to do on themselves. In her *Essence* magazine article 'Is all your money on your back?' bell hooks points out that women (black women in particular) are strongly susceptible to bourgeois consumerism.

> *'Money and clothes distort reality, making us vulnerable to many troubles. When we are obsessed with how we look, we place too much value on the surface and ignore the real work we must do to be truly beautiful.'* [30]

Judging from the proliferation of women's magazines and women's attachments to clothing, shoes, bags, perfume, expensive lifestyles, etc., women are the prime targets for advertising. By exploiting their longing for luxury, mass media tacitly encourage them to invest in or support capitalism.

Failure to confront the powerful forces that control women's behaviour in a world governed by men will reduce them to powerless beings incapable of freeing themselves from the addictions that come with intimate relationships, fame, power and its association with money provided by a man. Power that is fuelled by fear – fear of losing a man/woman, a job, a house, a car, fame, looks and your sense of self – is not worth fighting for. However, power that comes from a strong inner sense of self and a conscious decision to live a fulfilling life despite not having the material trappings that are so important to some people, is more sustainable in the long run but very difficult to cultivate.

'Who are you calling bitch?': a review of women as performers in rap music

Women entering the rap music industry as performers are, according to South African arts and culture writer Bongani Madondo, classified into two major categories, namely 'phly girl' or 'bitch' (depending on whether she toes the line or not) and tomboy. In the latter case, women try to match the men in their dress, wearing baggy pants with their underwear showing along the waistline, using foul language, smoking, drinking and pretending to be one of the boys even with the threat of possible physical and sexual assault by the boys themselves. In South Africa, the young Nomasonto Maswanganyi, aka Mshoza, burst onto the kwaito scene looking and trying hard to sound like the boys. Nowadays, however, she is seen sporting long relaxed hair, make-up and tight revealing clothing.[31]

In the United States, artists such as Missy Elliott (who went on to become an accomplished songwriter and producer) and MC Lyte are examples of women who subscribed to the tomboy persona. In 2005, Lil' Kim was reported to have been in trouble with the law for committing perjury and was celebrated for being the first woman in the hip-hop community to do jail time.[32] Lil' Kim and Foxxy Brown are examples of women who sing about receiving cash and gifts for sexual favours and trick men in the way they have been tricked by society. In this way, aberrant male behaviour is replaced by aberrant female behaviour. However, this role reversal does not bring with it any change in thought or perception.

As the industry evolved, the tomboy persona gave way to what Yvonne Bynoe refers to as a sexualised girl toy image.[33] This required women to lose weight, focus on their hair and make-up. To succeed in the industry, women had to recast themselves as divas. Looks became more important than skills and all a woman needed to do in order to succeed was, according to Da Brat, 'look fuckable'.[34]

Part of being a diva includes wearing revealing and tight-fitting clothes including constricting one's chest with an underwire bra to produce a dramatic cleavage. If a woman feels that she does not possess the right 'vital statistics', she may seek the help of a plastic surgeon (mostly white men) who will cut, push up and pull in body parts in all the right places. For many black divas, this means that they do not only have to subject themselves to the Western notion of beauty regarding hair texture, make-up and fashion. They also have to resort to a little help from a surgeon who will mould their bodies according to acceptable Western beauty prescriptions.

Not all women subscribe to the look described above. Similarly, not all women rappers try to match men by using profane language in their lyrics. When she emerged onto the scene in the early '90s, Queen Latifah opted for a modest Afrocentric look and chose lyrics to instil pride in black women. Her song 'U.N.I.T.Y.' challenged men's disrespect of women by asking the question: who are you calling bitch?

> *'Instincts lead me to another flow*
> *Every time I hear a brother call a girl a bitch or a ho*
> *Trying to make a sister feel low,*
> *You know all of that's got to go'*

In 'Ladies First' Queen Latifah uses the phrase 'there's going to be some changes in here' – an adaptation of Malcolm X's words. Kelly Ward asserts in her article 'Back That Ass Up' that by using the words of Malcolm X, Queen Latifah identifies with the broader struggle for equality within America yet, at the same time, she also chooses to place her call for equality within the feminist struggle.[35] By doing so, she encourages women, especially black women, to fight against racial discrimination and to confront the violence and sexual harassment they receive from all men, black and white.

Queen Latifah attempts to negate many of the female stereotypes such as the patriarchal view of sex mainly for purposes of men's pleasure, and also links women to divinity. There are many other women artists who opt to counter the sexist and violent content of rap. Even though some do not belong to the rap genre, women like Tracy Chapman, Jill Scott, Erykah Badu, Lauryn Hill and India Arie come to mind. Locally, women such as Miriam Makeba and Busi Mhlongo, and the younger generation including Zolani Mahola, Thandiswa Mazwai and Simphiwe Dana, present an image that inspires pride in who you are as an African woman – irrespective of body size and shape.

If not a bitch, then a witch

Widespread subjugation of women corresponds with their appropriation as sexual objects irrespective of whether the woman is a singer, writer, model, politician, lawyer or religious leader. This is a reflection of the fact that women are generally not respected at all. Why else would so many of women's personal boundaries and their rights be violated? Why is it okay to call someone a bitch but offensive to refer to another as a kaffir? What would happen if supporters (black and white) of the complainant in the Zuma rape trial carried placards outside the court building carrying the messages: Kick the Dog, Shoot the Kaffir, Kill the Wizard?

Somehow, it is acceptable to use derogatory names and labels such as motherfucker, witch, bitch and many others to refer to women. Even the ANC Youth League leader Fikile Mbalula is reported to have perfected his provocative sexist art by chanting slogans such as 'kill the witches'.[36] Mbalula's call to kill the witches is a reminder of the global witch hunt and murder of women that started in central Europe in the 14th century. Fuelled by the state and the church, female power became synonymous with evil and women were arbitrarily burned or hanged.

Publications such as *The Hammer of Witches* published by Catholic Inquisition authorities in 1485 and 1486 planted the seed of deep-seated and deranged global misogyny.

> *'What else is a woman but a foe to friendship, an unescapable punishment, a necessary evil, a natural temptation, a desirable calamity, an evil nature, painted with fine colours... Women are by nature instruments of Satan – they are carnal, a structural defect rooted in the original creation.'* [37]

A review of *Caliban and the Witch: Women, the Body and Primitive Accumulation* by Silvia Federici frames witch hunts as a strategy used by the Catholic Church (supported by nation states) to maintain law and order in times of social upheaval and change.[38] In this way, the church and the state tried to quell revolts by commoners and to control women's reproduction to ensure that sufficient pairs of hands would be produced to service future capitalist needs. Federici further argues that the church used witch hunts to terrorise independent women thinkers and rebellious colonial and slave subjects. Federici states that by representing women as witches or evil forces, working-class resistance to capitalist exploitation was divided and weakened.

As in Europe, witch-hunting in South Africa is a reflection of unstable socio-economic conditions and explosive political pressures. This explains why it reached its peak during the early 1990s when Nelson Mandela and other long-term political prisoners were released from prison. The situation continued into the new dispensation and it prompted the premier of the Northern Province, Ngoako Ramatlhodi, to appoint a commission of inquiry into witchcraft violence and ritual murders in 1995.

The Ralushai Commission found that even though men were also victims of witchcraft burning, the majority of victims were women.[39] Similarly, research carried out by the Commission on Human Rights and Administrative Justice in Ghana in 1998 found that over a thousand women and only 13 men were housed in witch refuges in northern Ghana.[40]

This gender dynamic is, according to Yaba Badoe, a scapegoat for social ills. Based on research that she undertook in witch refuges in Ghana, Badoe asserts that women who choose to live as free agents operating independently of male protection and control are often accused of being witches.[41] An economically and sexually independent woman, she argues, causes tremendous unease within the community in which she lives.

In South Africa it was not only witches who were burned to death in the late 1980s and early 1990s. Any man or woman accused of being an informer was attacked. Being accused of being a witch in a patriarchal and repressive society is as dangerous as being accused of being an informer in a politically charged and unstable environment. The time and money that was wasted on proving that Bulelani Ngcuka was not a spy is a classic example of how serious and life-threatening such accusations can be. The penalty for transgressing the attitudes and beliefs of the dominant political or gender regime is dangerous.

It is clear that in patriarchal society sources of negative energy are associated with women. This is well illustrated by the names and labels used to describe women. These labels are linked either to the devil or describe the reproductive or sexual role that women should play in relation to men. In my work with young people, we examine names and labels that are used to describe women compared to men in various languages (including tsotsi taal or *scamto*). I dare everyone to do the same exercise and analyse the origins and meaning behind such names.

One sunny Saturday morning I was driving through Soshanguve when I came to a four-way stop, facing a woman driver on the opposite side. A taxi approached from the left and should have waited for the woman to proceed as she had right of way. When she moved forward, the taxi moved forward too. Instead of stopping to let her proceed, the male driver stopped right in the middle of the intersection, opened the window and shouted insulting names that referred to her body parts. A group of women with their young children – boys and girls – were watching and listening at a nearby bus stop. What kind of example does this set for young men?

In an SAFM interview during the Zuma rape trial, a Zulu-speaking journalist said to his white colleagues, 'You should be glad you do not understand Zulu'. He said this in reaction to Zuma's supporters' never-ending chant of unprintable names referring to a woman and her mother's sexual body parts. Somehow, any woman who has given birth to a child can be called names by people that she will never meet in her lifetime. If you don't believe me, ask Zinedine Zidane's mother. Stuart Jeffries wrote in *The Guardian* that Marco Materazzi might have insulted Zinedine Zidane's mother during the World Cup. That, he argues, might seem as justification for the infamous head-butt. Why is it, Jeffries asks, that the worst insults in the world are always about your mother? [42]

As a woman of the 21st century, however, I choose not to throw up my arms in desperation asking the question: *Baba, senzeni na?* (What have we done?) Instead, I choose to raise my arms in gratitude ready to receive divine feminine and feminist opportunities ushered in by the era of the moment: the time for woman. More specifically, the time for African women has finally come. Those who still choose to wallow in a dream world and an illusion of their racial, gender and geographical superiority will catch up in their next lifetime.

'Women ask for it': from kangaroo court to kanga court

'This mama is speaking lies because she was in Zuma's room with that (kanga) on and he could see everything. After that Zuma slept with this mama and then she put the case against him. Zuma will win the case because this mama is speaking lies and all the people know it's wrong. She's got too much money and she didn't really work, where's this money coming from? This woman is an isigebengu (criminal), she is Zuma's girlfriend, otherwise why would she sleep with him without a condom.'

Sthembile Ndwandwe, single mother from Lamontville [1]

A ny South African who survived the country when it was on fire during the seventies and eighties will tell you stories about seeing people burned beyond recognition by mobs chanting slogans.

During this dark and horrible time in our country, anyone convicted of being a traitor by a kangaroo court was sentenced to a life of burning in hell. Even old men had to answer to boys presiding over kangaroo courts for offences such as not sleeping with their wives.

Many years after that period, South Africa came to witness a re-enactment of the kangaroo court mentality when people converged outside the High Court during Zuma's rape trial chanting slogans reminiscent of 'kill the witch, burn the traitor'. The man defending himself in the dock was not a traitor of the people but a champion of the liberation struggle. This man with his impeccable struggle credentials was in the dock not for blowing up racist military installations but was defending himself against rape charges.

Burning *impepho* (incense used by healers in cleansing ceremonies) and singing songs calling for the complainant's flesh and blood, the mob outside the court perceived the rape charge as an attack on their hero and resorted to a means of dialogue in which South Africans are well trained – sloganeering, intimidation, harassment and a blatant display of disobedience for anything or anyone perceived as authority. Later on, even old man Desmond Tutu was called to account for his sexual history by boys who are politically wet behind their ears and who seem to equate disrespect for their elders with freedom of expression. To them, a call for discipline (including self-discipline) as a critical means for decolonising the mind of Africans is dismissed as autocratic leadership.

Ironically, blaming and despising the complainant outside the court buildings was a reflection of the deliberations inside the court itself. Zuma's advocate, the learned Kemp J. Kemp, and the supporters blowing their *vuvuzelas* outside had one thing in common: they accused the complainant of inviting sex by wearing a kanga. In my view, Kemp's graphic interrogation of the complainant's past experiences of sexual intercourse carried the same message as a group of women burning panties outside the court.

The prevailing tendency to blame the oppressed for the consequences of their oppression is commonplace. It is the same attitude that blames a farm worker for bad body odour despite the fact that he not only works for a pittance but is housed with his family in a place that does not have running water and is situated miles away from the farm where he sweats for a living. For a woman accusing a man of rape, the same principle applies – she is blamed for something beyond her control.

From the moment she lays a charge of rape, her state of mind is in question. In his statement, Judge Willem van der Merwe said he allowed evidence to be led about the complainant's past sexual history because he wanted to explore evidence related to the complainant's mindset in terms of sexual matters.[2] However, Zuma's mindset regarding the alleged political conspiracy plot against him was never questioned.

It is hard enough for any individual to blow the whistle on fraud, corruption or any other criminal activity committed by those in power. However, a woman who chooses to blow a whistle of any sort, including laying a charge of rape against the Deputy President, has to be a woman of steel. This view is confirmed by Ama Ata Aidoo, who argues that a woman who takes action against her male comrades might hit a concrete wall with such force that she can never recover her original self.[3]

Blaming the woman is embedded in a specific patriarchal discourse that views women not only as inferior, but as evil and dangerous and a menace to society. Societal responses to sexual violence are influenced by myths, beliefs and stereotypes that emanate from such thinking.

Confronting myths about rape

People Opposing Woman Abuse (POWA) defines a myth as a commonly held belief or explanation of an event or phenomenon that is not true.[4] A myth arises from people's needs to make sense of acts that are senseless or violent. They try to explain horrible and violent phenomena such as rape and murder in ways that fit people's beliefs or preconceived ideas about life.

In his essay 'Debunking the Myths', Kalamu ya Salaam defines myths as traditional beliefs that are accepted uncritically.[5] Ya Salaam argues that even though many people may believe that myths are inherently false, some may even be true or have a historical basis. However, the main characteristic of a myth is that it is generally accepted as true without being questioned. The main reason for accepting myths at face value is that they either confirm what we want to believe or they reinforce collective ideas about how we see the world. The danger of myths is that they encourage people to conform to social illusions and to become self-fulfilling prophets of untested and unquestioned values. The main function of myths, according to Ya Salaam, is to stabilise the status quo by causing or encouraging conformity rather than challenging reality.[6]

While there are many myths about rape, I will only look at those that were played out in Jacob Zuma's rape trial.

1. A woman who lays a charge of rape is mentally ill
In the Zuma rape trial, Dr Louise Olivier, the forensic psychologist who testified for the defence regarding the complainant's state of mind, and other witnesses for the defence diagnosed the complainant as mentally ill.

It is not clear from the court proceedings when Zuma noticed the woman's alleged mental illness. Was it before or after the so-called consensual sex on 2 November 2005? It is a well-known fact that Zuma was close to the complainant's father. According to court records, she first met Zuma in Swaziland when she was about five years old. She remembers him from her early childhood as a very friendly uncle who was her father's close friend. Her father died in a motor accident in Zimbabwe in 1985.

The complainant was devastated by the death of her father. After her father's death, Zuma kept in contact with the family.

If Zuma kept in contact with the family, he would have been aware of the impact the complainant's father's death had on her mental state. He also would have been aware that the death (not to mention the rapes she was subjected to as a child) would have had an adverse impact on her mental wellbeing. If she was mentally ill before the alleged rape took place, she was not in control of all her mental faculties. Depending on when Zuma became aware of her illness, his decision to have sex with her was particularly ill-advised, especially if she initiated the sexual encounter, as he claims. By engaging with her sexually, Zuma acted like many other caregivers who care for disabled women and children financially but sexually assault them. This raises awareness about violence against disabled women in South Africa.

The extent of violence against disabled women is difficult to determine because service providers do not keep separate reports of the rape of disabled people. Similarly, there are no women's organisations or educational campaigns that are specifically aimed at women with disabilities. For instance, information about rape prevention is neither discussed among the deaf community nor distributed in Braille among the blind. Hotline counsellors are not trained to serve disabled women nor do they have the skills to provide counselling and support for disabled women. The women's movement has been particularly vocal about violence against able-bodied women but has not directed information specifically at disabled women. There is, therefore, a need for national research and action on this issue.

In the Zuma trial, the fact that the court declared the complainant to be mentally ill does not automatically render her incapable of distinguishing rape from consensual sex. The transformation of oppression into an illness is a well-known tactic that has been used by the courts, medicine, religion and culture. Institutions of power suppress voices of dissent by labelling people who challenge the status quo as mad, unstable, irrational or unbalanced. Because we all want to be perceived as balanced and 'rational' we may be afraid of voicing opinions that are contrary to popular belief or practice. Women living in a men's world become preoccupied with being logical to the point of suppressing alternative views. This, combined with women's low self-esteem and pressure to excel 'like men', makes having an alternative view or challenging patriarchy deeply distressing. In this instance, the woman's report of a sexual violation was seen as a personal pathology and used to exonerate the male oppressor. This is a key tactic of patriarchy and it is found in all sectors of society. It is meant to ensure that women remain silent and frozen. This fear is a necessary condition for the maintenance of male power over women.

Transforming oppression into an illness and the suppression of women's legitimate anger against gender violence is illustrated in an interview the complainant gave after Judge Van der Merwe pronounced his verdict:

> '*I haven't spoken out before because I did not want to be part of the game I saw happening through the media. I see myself being described and defined by others, the media, the defence, the judge. I have heard the things said by members of various structures and parties. I see analysis and judgments from all sides...*
>
> *Now I am angry and ready to speak. It is an anger with direction. I am ready to use it to take on the huge battle we have in our society when it comes to how women are viewed and treated and the kind of roles men play to keep women in these positions.*
>
> *I am not mad. I am not incapable of understanding the difference between consensual and non-consensual sex. The fact that I have been raped multiple times*

does not make me mad. It means there is something very wrong with our world and our society.' [7]

2. Women ask for rape by the way they dress

Control of women's clothing is essentially in the hands of men. From fashion designers to priests and traditionalists, men decide how women should appear in public and in private. The politics of dress has less to do with what women want to wear and more to do with what men would like women to believe is right for them.

A conflict exists between contemporary fashion designers who are hell-bent on creating modern clothing that reveals a woman's 'sexy' body for men's pleasure, while religious and cultural rules oppose a woman's 'pure' body being revealed so that they can neutralise her potential for seducing a man. Women's choices of clothing, like many other factors in life, are influenced by socio-cultural, religious and political mores and the current global socio-economic order. Most of the women on the catwalks and red carpets of Milan, Paris, London and New York are dressed by male fashion designers.

Dress is also used to construct and express national identity and respect for African culture. A kanga with the smiling face of Robert Mugabe or King Mswati around a woman's curves, or semi-nude participation in the reed dance in Swaziland and KwaZulu-Natal, sets the trend. In other cases dress is used to indicate that the wearer belongs to a certain religion. Women may wear veils, long dresses or head wraps.

It doesn't seem to matter what type of clothing women wear, they are all equally susceptible to being raped. Rape is a pre-meditated crime; it can happen to any girl or woman irrespective of whether she is in a nappy, fully covered on her way from collecting her pension, wearing an elegant suit working late at night in her office, dancing semi-nude in a nightclub or fully clothed taking care of her children at home. Controlling women's clothing does not have the goal of reducing rape because it does not require men to take responsibility for their sexual decisions and actions.

In the case of Zuma rape trial, the myths related to a woman's dress included comments about the complainant wearing a skirt and not pants, and later changing into a kanga. The myth of the miniskirt has been addressed in gender circles and in the media. One such article was by Justice Malala, who eloquently wrote in the *Sunday Times* about his encounter with a miniskirt when he was 17.[8] However, Malala's encounter with a miniskirt was not in person but in the form of an educational pamphlet highlighting black women's triple oppression as woman, black person and worker. Malala recounts that during those days a man accused of rape stood a chance of being acquitted if he alleged that the woman was dressed in a provocative manner. According to cultural beliefs and the law (which always seem to work together when it comes to controlling women's sexuality), a woman wearing a miniskirt is asking for rape.

Aside from being put on trial because of wearing a skirt, the complainant in the Zuma trial was also accused of wearing a kanga. Both are reported to have sent a sexual message to the Deputy President, who, being the law-abiding citizen he is, took it upon himself to act accordingly.

A kanga is a rectangular piece of cotton cloth that originated in East Africa. The original design was called *leso*, after the handkerchief squares that inspired its creation. Later on, its buyers (mainly men who bought it as a gift for their wives) named the cloth *kanga* after the noisy and sociable guinea-fowl known for its elegant, spotty plumage.[9] Kanga designs evolved from the spotty design to a variety of bold designs and bright colours.

Later on in their evolution, Swahili proverbs were printed on kangas. The kanga became a useful communication tool. It is not clear whether the kanga the complainant wore on the night of the alleged rape had any clear sexual proverb written on it or whether the sexual message was a figment of Zuma's creative imagination.

A kanga is the width of an adult's outstretched arms and wide enough to cover an adult woman's body from above her breasts to below the knee. It is neither short nor tight and is designed to flow around a woman's contours. In addition to being used as a wrap for women's bodies, kangas have multiple functions including carrying babies, covering tables and decorating walls. Men are also reported to sleep in them and wear them around the house as wraps.[10]

Kangas also have political uses; they are in some parts of Africa what the T-shirt is to political campaigns in South Africa. While T-shirts are worn by both men and women, kangas are mostly worn by women. You will often see female political supporters wearing kangas emblazoned with their candidate's face dancing at political rallies.

In South Africa, the kanga has not become a popular tool for political campaigning. This might not be a bad idea for the Zuma camp to explore, given that a poll conducted by the *Sowetan* newspaper to determine support for Zuma becoming the country's next president revealed that he had more support amongst men than amongst women.[11] Should Zuma choose to adopt the kanga as a tool for political campaigning, I would recommend the Swahili message *msilale wanawake* (women don't sleep).

3. Women as property in African culture
Contemporary interpretations of African culture seem to equate women with cows or land that a man owns. She is accorded little or no respect and is perceived to be of lesser value. Her role in the world is limited to catering to men's basic human needs, including giving birth to children (preferably male) as a means of contributing to the multiplication and survival of the race.

What is a woman? What role does a woman play in African

society and what is the nature of her relationship with an African man? On 9 August 2005 (South African Women's Day), a group of women (myself included) gathered in a round thatched mud hut along the banks of the Hennops River to listen to *uBaba* Credo Vusamazulu Mutwa speak about what it means to be a woman in African society.

Mutwa started by paying tribute to African goddesses, queens and warrior women across Africa and in the Diaspora. His point of departure was to thank the goddess Nomkhubulwane, whom he regards as the first god – 'the one who unfolded creation'. He saluted the cat queen, Manthatise, and Queen Nzinga of Angola who fought against the Portuguese for 47 years and was never defeated. As she lay on her deathbed at an advanced age, she put her spear next to her and remarked that she had only been conquered by the greatest enemy – death.

Still paying tribute to women, Mutwa called on the spirit of Nandi who was instrumental in planning Shaka's military operations in minute detail. This included ensuring that there was food and medicine during the war. After Nandi's death, Mutwa reports, Shaka never won another battle. Mutwa's tribute to African women living in Africa moved beyond her borders to connect with the spirits of those who also invoke spirits of black gods in the distant hills of Asia, the Americas and New Zealand.

According to Mutwa, a woman is a great being. She is directly connected to the Moon. The connection between women and the Moon, Mutwa asserts, explains why women who live together or who are connected to each other spiritually often menstruate at the same time. Women are governed by deep spiritual powers of the universe. It is interesting that oral history and written texts about the rise of African religion and spirituality exclude the role that women have played and are playing in this arena.

Mutwa's views about the key and central role that women played in African spirituality are highlighted in a conversation between Desiree Lewis and Molara Ogundipe, a leading feminist author, poet and activist teaching and writing about African cultural and gender studies. Because of their connectedness to the gods, Ogundipe argues that in traditional societies, women were archives for indigenous knowledge. For instance, the Yoruba Ifa divination system with its history and mythology acknowledged women and the divine female principle.[12] Almost every male priest of Ifa, Ogundipe further argues, had to be backed by a 'powerful female who upholds the world', who served as his reference and resource person. Ogundipe asserts that the word 'woman' is sometimes translated as 'witch' in Yoruba everyday speech. In a sense, a witch is a woman who possesses indigenous knowledge and mysterious powers.[13] Indeed, closer to home, we all know of Queen Modjadji who possessed scientific rainmaking knowledge.

Because she comes from and treads in the footprints of the divine female principle, a woman is a guardian of truth. This explains why people swear by their mother when they give evidence (*ubufakazi*). As descendants of priestesses, women are custodians of deep secret knowledge. Their role includes, amongst other things, imparting compassionate teachings of the deep knowledge to their families.

In their role as custodians of great knowledge, women are supported by men, in particular the uncles of their children. An uncle (*umalume*), Mutwa explains, does not have to be related by blood lineage. Any mature and responsible man within a clan can be assigned the role of passing on sacred knowledge to boys. This includes sex education, which, in African culture, is not separated from the broader teachings of morality, justice and caring for oneself and others – *motho ke motho ka batho* (I am because you are). If children learn sacred knowledge from a caring and compassionate teacher who is one of their own, they tend to see the knowledge as part of their heritage and are careful not to abuse this knowledge.

Metaphorically, sex education is presented as crossing a deep and wide river. The focus is not only on learning to swim so that you don't drown but on how to become one with the river. Water is a source of life, an element used for cleansing, purifying and unifying. However, like any other element (fire, earth, air) water can give life, and it can take life. Using a river as a symbol in sex education relates to the ambivalent symbol of life and death, creation and destruction, as well as the opposites between feminine and masculine.

In my studies of sex education from elders in rural parts of South Africa, I have also learnt about a woman's body as an entity that is composed of oceans. This is expressed by the saying *mmele wa mme o na le mawatle*. These oceans encompass female ejaculate, menstrual blood, amniotic fluid and breast milk. These oceans symbolise the creation of life.

In his address, Mutwa expressed regret that currently our children receive sacred knowledge from strangers using strange mediums such as television. As a result, such knowledge is mere information. It is not part of sacred knowledge.

Some of the ancient teachings, according to Mutwa, are based on the following principles:

- Respect a woman. All women are your mother.
- Respect a child – *umkhonto ka Somandla* (children are a spear of God that landed on Earth).
- Respect your brother, he is of one spirit.
- Create peace and love in communion with others.

According to Mutwa, it was women who recognised plants as food and medicine. They also invented bags to carry grain – *umfazi u faza imbewu*. This means that women contribute to the process of enhancing rather than taking away life. Mutwa reports that African women were amongst those who bought farms in the Transvaal in the 1930s. Even though many were poor as a result of apartheid, they had ideas and created saving schemes such as *umathelisana*, which infuses the principle of *ubuntu* into economic empowerment strategies.

Mutwa also argued that a man is the head of the household but the woman is the heart. Both the head and the heart have to work together to create harmony and balance. Both are necessary for life and living; if one dies, there's no life. Responding to the high level of violence against women in our communities, Mutwa explained that in Zulu rape is referred to as *ukudlwengula*, which means 'to tear apart'. Every time a man rapes a woman, he not only rips her body and soul apart, he also cuts the connection of a people to the Spirit. In the same way, Sotho phrases that explain rape, i.e. *go betella* or *go kata*, express ways in which the Spirit is suppressed and buried, which makes it impossible for the Spirit to breathe life into our collective soul.

Mutwa's views on rape are supported by another elder, Drake Kgalushi Koka, who led the first men's march against rape in Alexandra Township that was organised by ADAPT in May 1997.

> 'We can never build our country with violence. We can never build our country with car hijackings. We can never build our country with rape. There has been enough bloodshed in this country. As African people, we will not go against the teachings of our ancestors. We will respect our mothers, our sisters, and bless our daughters.' [14]

Speaking of love and marriage, Mutwa emphasised that love is like a plant, it needs to be nurtured or it will die. One way of making sure that love stays alive, he said, is to make your wife your best friend. As best friends, man and woman evolve together and separately, and are bound by love. In describing his marriage to Cecilia, his late wife, Mutwa said that as a healer, he could not view his wife as a sexual object. Rather, he committed to a marriage of intellect and artistic creativity. Mutwa urges men to be secure enough to free their wives to fly like falcons, to allow them to participate in ceremonies far away from home without feeling jealous. A bird that is free always flies back to the warmth and comfort of its nest.

The lessons learnt on that Women's Day confirmed that African women are no-one's property. Rather, they are special creations and custodians of truth, love, peace and deep spiritual knowledge. Through her, the rest of the family and community are connected to the Spirit – *umfazi umavula indlela*. After hearing Mutwa's address I realised that African women have no idea of how beautiful, intelligent, resourceful and deeply connected they are with the Great One. Foreign culture and religion have cut African women's connection with God.

Sacred knowledge is slowly being resurrected in different sectors and there is a call for African women to re-think their responses to societal crises. Jovial Rantao was right to be shocked about the number of Zuma's female supporters who chanted profanities outside the court building.

> 'You had to have been on this cobbled Johannesburg pavement and looked at the expressions on their faces and into their eyes. Then you would have experienced the emotion, hatred and commitment to their cause – horrible as it may sound. When you listen to their voices, and the insults spluttering out of their mouths at breakneck speed hit home, their true meaning would leave you feeling sick and angry.
>
> The young woman they called "bitch" is a human being. She is someone's daughter, someone's friend, someone's relative and, most of all, she should be a fellow human being to those who have displayed such forceful hatred.' [15]

Rantao's last statement couldn't be further from the truth. What is it that this woman has done to make other women act in a manner that is so insulting to womanhood? What is it that she has done that makes women resort to fire (a masculine element) when they could have used water (a feminine element) to bring balance to a crisis that is ripping our country apart?

It is interesting that it was Adriaan Vlok who used the symbolism of water by washing Frank Chikane's feet as a way of asking for healing, forgiveness and reconciliation. Symbolically water, or the feminine principle, is a key element on the cosmological wheel. According to some people, water is critical for cooling the raging fires to bring stability and re-orient cosmic energies with community and continuity.[16] Drought, as we all know, has the potential to kill all living organisms. A spiritual drought also kills. However, the effects of spiritual death manifest in subtle and invisible ways.

In African religions, people are healed by drinking water mixed with *sewasho* – ash. *Sewasho* is not an ordinary ash; it is prepared in a fire ritual. In his book *The Healing Wisdom of Africa*, Malidoma Somé describes fire as a force that makes us do, see, feel, love and hate.[17] It has the power to make us feel intense compassion or intense hate. Positive fire, he argues, emerges in the form of visions, dreams and intimacy with the ancestors, while negative fire presents itself in the form of speed, restlessness, the radical consumption common in modern society, and physical and spiritual death. Somé goes on to say that the fiery temperament of contemporary society is a result of being misaligned with fire. The fire is raging out of control and we are experiencing war and conflict across the world, pursuit of material goods and a lack of respect for life. *Sewasho* is prepared in a ritual of using fire that is meant to reconnect with the ancestors. In the ritual, herbs are burned. Herbs represent plants and the life that comes from the Earth. Earth rituals heal people's sense of belonging, self-worth and community.

159

'Our womb is the earth; it is our place of origination.
Feelings of absence, of being out of touch, any form of
alienation, anonymity and purposelessness – all are
symptomatic of a disconnection with the earth. No
other element can heal the hollow psyche in search of
fulfillment...' [18]

When mixed with water, *sewasho* encompasses the elements of earth, fire, air and water. My first experience of participating in a fire ritual of preparing *sewasho* shattered my Western comfort zones. Wearing a silk skirt, I spent a day in the scorching sun around the fire with my healer aunt collecting wood and burning herbs and medicinal plants.

My silk skirt snagged on one thorny bush after another. By the end of the day, I was tired, hot and tight-lipped, my hands bleeding and burning from being pricked by thorns whilst my aunt continued to sing peacefully throughout the ceremony. It came as a relief when we went home at dusk to know that I couldn't greet or speak to anyone otherwise I would be expected to repeat the entire ceremony the next day. Frankly, after the experience, I was in no mood for a chat with anyone.

As custodians of sacred knowledge and weavers of community and continuity, African women are called to be mindful of how they relate to their families, communities and the world. While it is important that African women are supportive and protective of their men and children, this should be done in a way that is not detrimental to their health and wellbeing. It is true that African women cannot afford to give up on African men. After all, their spiritual liberation is intertwined.

However, standing by men is not the same as remaining silent and not taking a stand against men when they act in a manner contrary to the ancient practice of respecting women's humanity and integrity. While it is important to seek interventions that reconcile rather than divorce the African woman from men, this should not be done in a way that is detrimental to the physical, psychological and spiritual wellbeing of women.

The first step is for African women to focus on their primary relationships (their relationships with themselves) and rebuild a loving, caring and nurturing relationship with their bodies and their souls. It is only when African women feel good and centred in their identity that they can contribute meaningfully to a review of their relationships with men. Creating alternative modes of self-love will, in some instances, break away from tradition. This includes replacing negative views of African femininity with positive thought and action.

To illustrate, the application of the concept of 'motherism' in African feminism should not be used to keep women within the confines of their biological functions. Interpretations of proverbs such as *mmangwana o tshwara thipa ka fa bogaleng* (literally, 'woman holds the knife at the sharp point' – meaning that as a mother, a woman gives her life to her husband and children) focus on the value of self-sacrifice that society expects from a woman. This value in itself is not negative. However, when it is enforced in an unequal society, it limits the woman's potential to pioneer alternative modes of gender relations and leadership within and outside the home.

Similarly, African men need to find time and create space to heal their wounds rather than taking out their pain on women. In his essay 'Redefining Masculinity in a Changing World', Frank Meintjies asks the questions: what is a man? What is manhood?

'We all think that manhood is a great thing. On the outside, this manhood looks tough and powerful yet is fragile, false and comes with a lot of pain. Confounded by the belief that men don't cry, many of us shy away from feeling our pain. Feeling our pain and shedding our tears as men represents a road to our recovery, to our true manhood.

When you do something that hurts other people, instead of being strongly condemned, society might encourage you. If you cheat women, undermine them or even abuse them, other men will not stand up against you... As we get together for a drink in pubs, when we call women bitches and whores, other men will not condemn the behaviour. For men, our identity as males is shaped by the sexist reality into which we were born. That reality includes exerting power over others, particularly women.' [19]

Meintjies goes on to explain that the kind of masculinity described above robs men of the ability to feel, particularly the ability to give and receive love.

'Very often, we push away people who want to be close to us. I am sure that many women know how difficult it is to work out what is going on in the mind of the man they are with. Often, we hide behind a newspaper and when we are asked what is wrong, we reply "nothing". As a result of this, we move into isolation and find ourselves alone... The thing about love is that you have to open yourself, you have to take the risk of being vulnerable.' [20]

An inability to give and receive love is not limited to men. From my personal relationships with men and my work, I know that modern women also struggle with this issue. Many of us wear our wounds like impenetrable armour and carry them from one relationship to another and experience relationships as battlegrounds for power in a male–dominated world. Women's inability to love in modern society can also be compounded by living in a consumerist culture that equates expressions of love with receiving expensive gifts and not with simple acts of care.

Humans have come to view vulnerability and humility as a sign of weakness. We hope and pray that African women and men will rediscover each other's souls and reclaim their innate ability to give and receive love. Perhaps in time African women and men will cultivate a commitment to love, compassion, and intellectual and spiritual companionship. In time, African men and women might find time in their busy BEE lives to hold hands and recite the poem 'I Love Myself the Way I Am' by Jai Josef, a Native American spiritual healer and poet:

> *'I love myself the way I am*
> *There is nothing I need to change,*
> *I'll always be the perfect me,*
> *There is nothing to rearrange.*
> *I'm beautiful and capable of being*
> *The best I can,*
> *And I love myself just the way I am.*
>
> *I love you just the way you are,*
> *There's nothing you need to do*
> *When I feel the love inside myself,*
> *It's easy to love you.*
> *Behind your fears, your rage and*
> *Tears, I see your shining star.*
> *And, I love you just the way you are.'* [21]

Another relationship that requires review is the one between black and white women. The tension emanating from race and class privilege has not been adequately addressed within the context of violence against women in South Africa. It is a tension that was raging behind the scenes during the Zuma trial.

In many ways, white women still operate as the architects of theory and practice for many organisations working in the area of women's empowerment, in the arena of violence against women in particular. Because they had access to quality education and resources, white women activists have a status that is different from that held by black women activists. In this way, they remain better positioned to influence policies, legislation, programmes and strategies geared towards addressing violence against women. A perusal of published material in this sector attests to this fact. White women have the skills to undertake research and publish; as a result there are few black women doing the same in the movement. Instead, they remain the subjects of research.

In her article 'The Right to Self-determination in Research', Dabi Nkululeko asks the question: can a segment of an oppressed group rely on knowledge produced, researched and theorised by others, no matter how progressive they are?[22] Nkululeko's article was written in 1987. Not much has changed since then. The agenda of addressing and responding to gender violence in black communities does not lie in the hands of black women and men. The anti-rape movement in South Africa is still led by white women. While many of them are doing a splendid job in supporting black women in dire situations, why is it that they remain the only ones who write and speak for black women and men?

What does research on masculinity mean when most of the subjects are black men from the ghetto and villages who are responding to research questions posed by white scholars, both male and female? What does this mean for a redefinition of African feminism? What does this mean for re-weaving the threads that make up the black family which have been torn apart by racial, class and cultural imperialism?

Developing paradigms that regard white culture as the main event and relegate indigenous wisdom to the fringes is an expression of latent colonialism. This situation has serious implications for the production of knowledge within the women's movement in South Africa. Knowledge is power. If knowledge production is reserved for the privileged few, the situation does not augur well for correcting the imbalance of power between black and white women. It is critical that a pool of African women leaders should be formed at political and economic levels, within academia and civic movements, and in communities so that they can create financial and technical support mechanisms to enable African women document their own stories.

In her 1987 article, Nkululeko warns that we should not overlook the fact that sometimes native researchers, like their Western counterparts, have to unlearn their privileges. She too may have inherited the ideological trappings of her class, which may not be in line with the everyday life experiences of the majority of women who are discriminated against in their communities. Because she is alienated from her cultural heritage, she too may use tools that are based on colonial scholarship.[23]

Currently, African women's strategies, that are geared towards creating peace in their lives and those of their families cannot only depend on Western strategies which, as we all know, have failed many an abused woman and child. It is critical that strategies should include ways of restoring the souls of African men and women. Moral regeneration cannot happen without a renewal of the soul. The renewal of the soul follows a path that cannot be legislated for in parliament or studied at a prestigious university. It is a way of finding the spark that will trigger a loving and compassionate way of being with who we are after having been told that we are of no substance and value.

One way of reclaiming who we are is through confronting the prevailing stereotypes about blacks, women and men. For example, upholding the notion that black men are incapable of controlling their sexual desires is a tragedy for the whole nation.

In an article about Zuma and the ANC in *Business Day*, Karima Brown and Vukani Mde state that 'men who find themselves without a condom at the precise moment it is needed, go right ahead anyway, placing themselves and their partners in danger'. The article also argues that it is important for South Africans to overcome personal denial about the HIV/Aids pandemic and that we should speak honestly and openly about the 'political denial that gives our personal behaviour a veneer of respectability'.[24]

As *umalume* who is given the responsibility of passing on sexual teaching from one generation to the next, Zuma's comments about Zulu culture and sex must not be taken lightly in a country where many young boys do not have fathers or elders to teach them, and depend on TV for knowledge about life and living. As a leader and an elder who is passionate about his country and his culture, as a father who is equally passionate about the future of his children's children, it is incumbent on Zuma to ask for guidance and reverse the negative effects of his false teachings. A rushed apology at a press conference on his way to sing *Umshini wam* at a rally in a nearby stadium is definitely not the path to the soul.

4. Rape is a crime of passion

The belief that men rape because they cannot control themselves sexually is a myth based on the belief that once they are aroused, men cannot help themselves. This means that once a man gets past the 'point of no return' he cannot do anything but penetrate a woman's body and is unable to exercise restraint and control over his sexual urges.

In her book *Forgiveness and Other Acts of Love*, Stephanie Dowrick highlights the value of restraint in our lives. Restraint, she argues, is an act of will; the expression of deciding for yourself.[25] At points in our lives, we are faced with many paths and decisions we have to make. The difficulty of making the right choice is often exacerbated by the speed with which life flies by in contemporary society. Every second and every day, we are bombarded with information from the media (audio, electronic, print), telephones, e-mail and endless meetings.

This information overload and the demands of modern life put us under immense pressure to make instant choices.

This state of affairs affects people's ability to reflect, which in turn affects their capacity to exercise restraint. Reflection is a necessary condition for clarity and influences the choices we make. Reflection gives restraint room to grow, which in turn becomes an expression of intention.

> *'Restraint offers a space between intention and action...*
> *The more conscious you are of that space, and the*
> *freer you are to occupy it more easily, you can choose*
> *whether and how to act.'* [26]

Dowrick argues that restraint cannot be practised without some degree of maturity.[27]

Rather than behaving like children who thrive on instant gratification, mature adults have to learn to engage their impulses (sexual or otherwise) in the most sober manner. Refusing to be responsible for our actions is not only an immature act but a refusal to be fully human. Denying our mistakes and acting as though they did not happen or were caused by others deprives us of the human element. No-one is perfect but we have to acknowledge this and not ignore it.

When he was charged with rape and corruption, Zuma blamed other people for his actions. In his corruption trial he blamed people behind the alleged conspiracy plot to oust him from the presidential race, and in the rape trial he blamed the complainant for wearing a skirt and a kanga as well as sending him 'signals' that she wanted to have sex with him. By doing this Zuma portrays himself as a powerless slave to sexual provocation and a helpless victim of outside forces.

We all have to learn to practise restraint every day so that we can prevent ourselves from committing endless mistakes that require public and private apologies. Restraint is a source of inner power necessary to free humans from reacting to situations out of habit. For men this includes debunking prevailing myths about women and sex.

As indicated earlier, one of the greatest problems hampering rape and HIV/Aids prevention is the belief that men cannot control themselves if they are aroused. The myth equates sex with an act of violence. Rape is not a sexual act but an act of violence that uses sex as a weapon. It is motivated by aggression and men's desire to control and exercise power over women. Patriarchal masculine power is at its core and it is transmitted through the ways in which boys and men relate to women and their bodies. This applies to all men irrespective of race, class, religious, cultural and educational backgrounds.

Because they are socialised into a sexist society, many men get away with rape. Sadly, some do not even view what they do to women as rape. This is how Nathan McCall describes his initiation into the world of women and sex:

> *'At about the tender age of sixteen, I carried around in my wallet a wrinkled piece of paper that contained a notorious list. I'm ashamed to admit it now, but back then I proudly showed off the contents of that list, often during wine-bingeing bragging sessions with the boys on the block.*
>
> *The list contained the names of some twenty or so teenage girls — in our vernacular, babes, broads, bitches — who held the unlucky distinction of having been laid by me.'* [28]

McCall states that even though the incident described above happened many years ago, this mentality still prevails in modern society. He argues that men don't really understand the tragic implications of their sexual behaviour towards women. To them, it is merely an expression of their power.

'From this male perspective, the pervasiveness of men's problems with sexual aggression suggests one or two things: either God developed a defective sensibility gene when he assembled males, or there's a major flaw in our cultural conditioning, and that flaw feeds this madness that's corrupted us.

After much soul-searching, I'm inclined to believe the latter is true; that even in these so-called modern times, we still uphold a supermacho cultural climate that helps men feel comfortable – even justified – in forcing their attentions on the opposite sex. Certainly, the role of individual responsibility can't be dismissed but in a sense our whole society is an accessory in this thing called rape.' [29]

It is true that rape is most prevalent in cultures that demonstrate little or no respect for women's rights; a culture whose ethos includes violence as an expression of manhood. We know that rapists don't rape for sexual pleasure or because they cannot have sex elsewhere. Many are involved in regular relationships with women. Rapists rape to feel powerful and in control in the same way that a powerful country uses violence against another to impose its will.

To rape a woman, a man has to dehumanise her and regard her as a lesser human than himself. However, anyone who regards someone as a lesser human has feelings of being dehumanised himself. The self-destructive nature of some men is highlighted by Bell Hooks in her book *The Will to Change*. She argues that the first act of patriarchy demands that men should engage in acts that kill their emotions, i.e. acts of 'psychological self-mutilation'.[30] One of the rewards for obeying patriarchal thought and practice, she argues, is the right to dominate women sexually, and if females are not available (e.g. in prison), a man can place a weaker male in the 'female' position.

To further illustrate cultural conditioning of male domination, Robert Jensen outlines ways in which sex is described in a sexist society. Jensen notes that the slang term for sexual intercourse, fuck, is used differently in different situations.

> *'To fuck a woman is to have sex with her. To fuck someone in another context ("he really fucked me over on that deal") means to hurt or cheat a person. And when hurled as a simple insult ("fuck you") the intent is denigration and the remark is often a prelude to violence or the threat of violence. Sex in patriarchy is fucking. We live in a world in which people continue to use the same word for sex and violence...'* [31]

A gay man who has chosen to abstain from patriarchal sex and pursue alternative ways of loving, Jensen argues that sexist beliefs about sex apply to both gay and straight men. In his opinion all men receive, to some degree, the same training and they respond to life from the dominator power model. In his call for the inclusion of intimacy, love, trust and respect between people, Jensen notes that sex is often described in terms of heat – for example hot babe, hot hunk, sizzling hot sex. In response to the heat generated by sex, Jensen asks the question:

> *'But what if our embodied connections could be less about heat and more about light? What if instead of desperately seeking hot sex, we searched for a way to produce light when we touch? What if such touch were about finding a way to create light between people so that we could see ourselves and each other better? If the goal is knowing ourselves and each other like that, then what we need is not heat but to light the path.'* [32]

The greatest challenge facing society is finding ways of dismantling the sexist notions of power over weaker people – be it other men, women, children, or other races or tribes. Searching for ways in which men and boys can resist being dominated and stopping the domination of others is particularly important.

Moving beyond re-educating individual men and boys in families, school, church, the workplace and other social agencies and including a review of larger systems of exploitation and oppression that make violence acceptable at national and global level is equally important. Formulating concrete and practical means of resisting systems of exploitation is certainly one of the greatest challenges facing men and boys in the 21st century. Similarly, it is critical for women and men to work together in developing partnership models based on mutual respect and compassion.

Almost all male activists and writers concerned about the escalating levels of violence against women call for a reconnection with the humane male psyche. Whilst acknowledging that men's violence could be a consequence of childhood experiences of violence, Zakes Mda questions male pain and argues that men must create spaces to heal so that they can, in time, experience the fullness of loving and living.

> 'We need to learn that compassion is not a sign of weakness. In time, when we have evolved into better human beings, we shall know how to cry not only because of pain but because of beauty too. Being able to cry because something is so beautiful that it moves you to tears is, in my opinion, a mark of greatness.' [33]

After the verdict, what next? Justice as part of the moral and spiritual healing agenda

> 'We need to re-evaluate our value system as a
> society. The highly competitive environment
> we have created and the resultant conflict and
> pressure on different sections of our society
> make post-apartheid black society seem like
> a car travelling at high speed, changing gears
> without any transmission oil. We need to stop
> for a moment and check the oil before the car
> breaks down completely.'

Sello wa Loate [1]

Vices turned into virtues

Money cannot buy love, so they say. What money *can* buy is the illusion of being loved, all the while living with a hollow feeling in your heart while you keep your eye on the ball – the material prize that comes with the illusion of love.

Can money buy justice? It cannot, it can only buy a plea bargain, an acquittal or some other related technical legal outcome. Following Judge Herbert Msimang's decision to strike Jacob Zuma's corruption case off the roll, Zuma's co-accused, Pierre Moynot, a French citizen employed by Thint Holdings, a multinational company that makes a living out of selling weapons, remarked that his company had always believed in the South African justice system.

This is in stark contrast to how many young, black South African men, who are crammed like sardines into overcrowded prisons and who are convicted of or are awaiting trial for petty crimes, feel about justice in their country. Even more devastating is that many of these young men will fall prey to gruesome gang rape while in prison. There is no denying that rape, of a man or woman, erodes a person's sense of self. For a country in which the majority of the population suffers from low self-esteem as a result of colonial conquest, this is fatal for future generations.

I wrote this last chapter the morning after Judge Herbert Msimang's decision to strike Zuma's corruption case off the roll. Listening to the contrasting views of Zwelinzima Vavi of the Congress of South African Trade Unions and Makhosini Nkosi of the National Prosecuting Authority over the radio, I stopped dead in my tracks to ask the question: is it worth publishing this book? In response, a resounding 'yes' reverberated through my being.

I indicated in the first chapter that I believe Jacob Zuma's saga reflects what is going on in the country and the world. The noise surrounding his court cases is a call to examine the deeds of African leaders at a time when the continent is expected to rise above its previous corrupt thoughts and acts. When he addressed his supporters outside the court following Judge Msimang's decision, Zuma reiterated his position – 'I said in the beginning that I did not do anything wrong, I still repeat this today.' In all his speeches, he has never said that he did the right thing, only that he did nothing wrong.

Not doing wrong is relative. During apartheid, resorting to armed struggle might have been wrong but it was the right thing to do considering the life-threatening situation that faced the majority of people in South Africa. What measure do we use to define what is right or wrong today? Wrongdoing seems to be relative in a democratic society where success is determined by access to material and political power, a society whose young people look up to a local drug lord driving the latest luxury automobile as a role model.

In 1997 whilst working as a founding director of Agisanang Domestic Abuse Prevention and Training (ADAPT), I commissioned a study on violence-related deaths in the lives of young men in Alexandra Township. The study, undertaken by Sello wa Loate, was based on three critical assertions:[2]

- Restoring self-love and pride in young black men is essential if violence against women is to be effectively addressed.
- Identifying key and effective strategies is essential for re-orienting socially dysfunctional and misdirected young black men as opposed the view that sees them as a lost generation.
- Reactivating the belief that young black men's place is not in prison and that they, like all of us, have a positive role to play in our society.

One of the respondents indicated how difficult it is for him not to steal, not to disrespect women and not to be violent. In his words, children are told by adults to be good while they (adults) live a life that sends the message that it is profitable not to be good.

Other voices that came out of the study were:

- 'In the past during the liberation struggle, we used to say power to the people. Nowadays, our leaders say power to the stomach.'
- 'We are used to seeing people die in our townships. That is a common feature of our lives. We no longer fear death and we also have little respect for life.'
- 'In the ghetto, all good people are poor, the criminals are successful.'
- 'The people we look up to are the ones who encourage us to steal, including our teachers.'

It is clear from the study that the government does not lead by example and that revelations of fraud and corruption show that addressing crime and corruption is a futile exercise because 'everyone is doing it'.

On the day of Judge Msimang's decision, I received a long-distance call from a friend who was alone at home in the evening, depressed, not by the court outcome, but by her inability to live her truth. She said: 'Everyone at work was rejoicing about the court outcome and I had to pretend that I agreed with them. Now that I'm home, I'm hit by my truth and I feel very depressed. Does it mean that those of us who are loyal and law-abiding civil servants struggling to make ends meet with low salaries are fools? Is it not better to join them since we cannot beat them?' I responded by quoting yet another friend with whom I had spoken earlier in the day. He said, 'We should never lose the voice of reason' irrespective of whether Jacob Zuma becomes president or not. Failure to live up to our values and principles, he said, is tantamount to mass suicide.

Let me make it clear that this book is not intended to thwart Jacob Zuma's dreams of becoming president of this country. If he is destined to lead the country, he will. Nothing and no-one will stop him. However, 12 years after the first democratic elections we should focus our attention on the quality of the leadership we deserve rather than the identity of the leader.

In their article about Zuma and the ANC, Karima Brown and Vukani Mde assert that if objections to Zuma being president are about criminality, they should fall away after his acquittal from the rape trial. However, if the objections are about moral judgment and personal wisdom, it is doubtful whether many people in the ANC's leadership would make the grade.[3] Brown and Mde go on to urge citizens to hold all leaders accountable to a set of standards that include honesty, integrity in both personal and public affairs, empathy, decisiveness and the gravitas to command respect at home and abroad. These standards, they argue, must apply universally to all leaders without fear or favour.

We live in dangerous times. The world is in the hands of corrupt capitalists parading as philanthropists. Similarly, corrupt criminals leading governments and religious institutions across the world hold the will of the people at ransom using their money, popularity and their weapons to crush any voice of dissent.

Many people would say it's a sign of the times; I say it's the sign of a passing phase that is moving from an old to a new energy. This phase will pass as people will not tolerate governance that lacks truth and honesty. Leaders' shady undercover operations will be exposed for all to see and learn from.

Personally, I am not vehemently opposed to having Jacob Zuma as my future president. Each of us has the ability to connect with our inner light and lead with truth or succumb to the trappings of our ego and lead people astray. It is for this reason that I'm interested in knowing that when Zuma is not in the company of his legal team and his loyal supporters, when he is alone with his spirit, what does his inner voice say to him? Can he hold my hand, look me in the eye as my leader and elder, and tell me the truth?

'Who does she think she is?' I hear you ask. As they say in township language, *Wie's jy? Jy's fokol. Ja, eintlik wie's ek?* (Who are you? You're fuck all. Actually, who am I?) If one uses contemporary material and political power as a yardstick, I wouldn't count for much. For instance, if I were to be hit by a truck, I would probably spend hours bleeding unattended on a stretcher in a public hospital simply because I cannot afford private health care. Were I to die from the accident, the administration of my estate would be easy and speedy and my children would have little to show by way of inheritance. As far as my struggle credentials go, I have never been arrested, never been in exile.

If I was to be convicted for mismanaging NGO funds, you can bet your last cent that when I go to prison, I will not be given a send-off by the who's who in politics. The probability of being served lunch by the minister of correctional services upon my arrival in prison is as strong as a heat wave in the North Pole. So, in the material and political world, I don't count for much. However, in another world, I am someone and I count. I am someone because I come from somewhere.

Rich or poor, politically popular or not, we all come from somewhere. We, Africans living on the southern tip of the continent, have come a long way. However, in spite of the achievements of the past few years, many of us are still haunted by the dark monster of rootlessness and loss of identity. This, as we know, is a result of our interaction with foreign cultures and the people who uprooted us from our own cultures.

African personhood and justice in contemporary society
According to Odora Hoppers, culture consists of socially transmitted behavioural patterns expressed through the arts, beliefs, religion, governance and other social agencies of human thought and practice.[4] Despite being central to our lives, culture is, unlike our DNA, not genetically transmitted. It is a learned construct passed on from one generation to another.

In contemporary South Africa, cultural knowledge is composed of cosmopolitan and traditional knowledge. However, the latter goes beyond wearing skins and feathers and dancing to the thump of a drum around a fire with a busload of tourists snapping away with their cameras. Traditional knowledge in Africa includes technologies that range from architecture, history, environmental conservation, ethno-mathematics, animal husbandry, medicinal knowledge, astronomy, governance and indigenous law.

All these disciplines recognise the importance of a connection between physical, social, psychological and economic paradigms and the body, mind and soul.[5] Unlike modern empirical paradigms that view life as a composition of disparate and disconnected entities, indigenous knowledge and culture view life as a holistic and interdependent relationship between the individual, family, community, nation and broader cosmos.

Sadly, African traditional knowledge is often reduced to singing and dancing and its significance is glossed over because some people feel it has no relevance to modern life. Indigenous economic thought should be integrated with economic empowerment in Africa but the ideas of indigenous people are disregarded as we continue to witness their displacement from their land to make room for national parks, military zones, mining companies and dam constructions.

From the Batwa of Uganda and Rwanda to the Baka of the Central African Republic, the San in Botswana to the Masai in Kenya, many people are evicted from their lands to make way for exploration and exploitation of their natural resources.[6] Over centuries, colonisers have perfected the art of territorial, intellectual and mental colonisation of the indigenous peoples of the world.

Uhuru Hotep argues that the colonisation process started with the invasion of Kemet (Egypt) by the Hebrews long after the pyramids were built.[7] Over time, the Assyrians, Persians,

Greeks, Romans, Arabs, Portuguese, Spanish, French, British, Dutch, Germans and Italians conquered Africa in what is referred to as the scramble for Africa, which reached its peak during the time of the infamous Berlin conference in 1886. By 1915, five minute European states – Britain, Holland, Germany, Portugal and France – had conquered the whole of Africa except for Ethiopia.[8]

Employing a process of miseducation, colonisers established schools that used a 'pedagogy and curriculum that deliberately omits, distorts or trivializes the role of African people in and their seminal contributions to world history and culture.'[9] It is through such education that Africans have come to identify with European history and culture while they remain ambivalent about or indifferent to their own. To this day, a view of African personhood is trapped in a cultural paradox that upholds the superiority of the European way of life.

It is in this light that Ayi Kwei Armah calls for African intellectuals to think independently and creatively instead of planning for a future that is based solely on imitating foreign empirical thinking.[10] Armah also warns against political agitation that is not preceded by a strong cultural education, which is in turn based on positive self-knowledge. Expecting politicians to solve deep-seated African cultural identity problems is, according to him, rather short-sighted.

> *'Politics being the living art of the possible, good politicians are professionally partial to visions short enough to be realizable within a few years. This is not because politicians are just congenitally myopic. They are in a problem-solving occupation with short deadlines, and they rise or fall according to the strength of their base constituency. Constituencies of men and women living in the here and now normally want solutions to problems of the here and now, and the*

*nature of their occupation places politicians under a
pressing obligation to solve just those types of problems.
Short term.'* [11]

With their focus on the here and now, Armah argues that
politicians are not concerned with the unborn or with ancestors
who lived many years ago because babies and dead people do
not vote. Because they are concerned with winning the next
election and purchasing the latest presidential plane, politicians
have no time or regard for anyone who will have not have an
active and visible role to play in making sure that they are voted
into power. Armah calls for an active and visible cultural and
intellectual contribution from cultural workers and intellectuals
across Africa so that the long-term goal of liberating African
minds is not tied to a specific presidential term.

A robust contribution of indigenous knowledge is needed
in all intellectual disciplines, including the legal system.
Legislation in any country is built on the supreme law of the
country, the constitution. However, in many African countries,
the constitution emphasises national unity instead of recognising
the diverse cultural and linguistic realities of the population. [12] In
South Africa, however, even though the Constitution recognises
the cultural, religious and linguistic realities of diverse
communities, indigenous people's cultural beliefs and their role
in crime prevention do not yet play a big enough role in policy-
making in the country.

Because it is based on the superiority of European law,
the South African legal system does not take into account the
role that indigenous justice could play in addressing the moral
breakdown and high levels of crime in the country. To illustrate,
while it was commendable that Zuma testified in his native
language followed by Judge Van der Merwe's attempts to address
him in Zulu at the beginning of the judgment, the outcome of the
trial itself was largely influenced by technical evidence provided

by Western-trained experts – legal and medical practitioners, scientists, technicians and psychologists.

There is no doubt that the professionals mentioned above have a critical role to play in helping legal practitioners solve criminal cases. They apply their skills diligently to the process and are regarded as experts upon whom the judge or magistrate relies for the verdict. Their expertise is based on the dominant power of Western science, which is never questioned.

Judge Van der Merwe has this to say about Dr Louise Olivier, who testified on Zuma's behalf:

> 'Dr Louise Olivier is a registered clinical and counselling psychologist. It is not necessary to refer to her curriculum vitae. It is an impressive curriculum vitae.
>
> Dr Olivier treats patients from different culture groups in South Africa and has patients from countries such as Botswana, Uganda and Tanzania. In her doctoral thesis she inter alia worked on the development of a psychometric test regarding the evaluation of sexual functions and adaptation of adults in South Africa. This test has found acceptance and is now used in South Africa.' [13]

In his judgment, Judge Van der Merwe rejected Dr Merle Friedman's evidence on the basis that she, according to Dr Olivier, did not make use of available psychometric tests.

> 'What is, however, of some importance to me is that no psychometric tests were done to find out more about the complainant's personality.' [14]

It is my view that the judge based this decision on a legal technicality without considering the manner in which psychometric tests are constructed and applied in a gender- and race-oppressive world. Even more critical is the fact that in Africa personhood is relationally defined and cannot only be determined through isolated individual psychological attributes measured by tests based on a European world-view and life experience.

In most instances the suitability of an expert called to give evidence is based on educational qualifications that may be beyond reproach but do not take the complainant's culture into account. The expert may not speak the defendant's language or be sensitive to his or her cultural norms. It is assumed that because experts have a qualification that shows extensive educational and professional experience, they are well equipped to make pronouncements on behaviour that may have moral or cultural roots. Whether it was consensual or not, sex between Zuma and the complainant raises serious moral arguments that psychometric tests cannot resolve.

Dr Olivier's impeccable evidence based on her training as a forensic psychologist raises two concerns: the tendency of professionals to 'pathologise' behaviour and the ways in which scientific evidence can be used as a tool to oppress women. In her evidence, Dr Olivier concerned herself with the 'madness' of the female victim as opposed to the 'badness' of the male offender.

Implicit in this is a message that says to men that even though rape may be against the law, forcing yourself on a woman is not fundamentally wrong and is explained with excuses such as: 'According to my culture, I was taught never to leave a woman who is aroused otherwise I will be charged with rape' (Zuma). Satisfying a woman's sexual needs was not the issue in this case.

Zuma may have thought he was doing the complainant a favour by having sex with her. Judging from his responses to Prosecutor De Beer's questions, there is a chance that Zuma might have perceived himself as providing a 'service' to someone who he thought needed to be 'serviced'.

De Beer asked Zuma about the claim that the complainant had shown she had sexual interest in him when she came to visit him in his study while wearing only a kanga.

> *De Beer: 'So from all this, what did you think she was up to?'*
> *Zuma: 'Maybe she was trying to send a certain message to me.'*
> *De Beer: 'And what message was that?'*
> *Zuma: 'Maybe she is lonely and I can assist her.'*
> *De Beer: 'Lend a helping hand?'*
> *Zuma: 'Yes.'* [15]

When it comes to patriarchal sex, men's sexual pleasure is seen to be of greater significance than a woman's. Women's magazines frequently contain articles such as 'How to satisfy your man sexually' or 'How to make sure that your man does not stray' or 'How to survive your man's infidelity'. Zuma's statements and the articles we see in women's magazines are aimed at protecting the male sexual ego rather than enhancing a woman's sexual pleasure.

In her article 'Sexual Pleasure as Feminist Choice', Patricia McFadden highlights the suppression of women's bodies and their sexuality within a patriarchal culture. The notions of pleasure and choice are rarely mentioned except when their overall goal is satisfying a man's lust and desire.[16] It is worth noting that the open discussion of sex and sexuality in contemporary society is a result of the high cost of HIV/Aids rather than a reflection of the achievements of the global feminist struggle in the arena of women's sexuality. For many women, sexuality is still treated in a manner that upholds men's superiority over women.

'Women's movements organizing around issues of sexuality have recorded some successes with respect to

*legal reforms and service provision in the realms of
sexual health and reproductive rights, anti-violence
movements, and movements against various traditional
rites and practices. Yet we now find ourselves at a
moment in which gains of the last decades are currently
in danger of being set back by the dominant political
agendas of our time. The doctrinaire and militaristic
global politics fomented by the Bush regime are
characterized by such deep sexual conservatism that
the prospects for any kind of sexual democracy once
again look thin.'* [17]

The conservative militaristic global regime has resulted in
war and women's bodies have also been caught in the crossfire.
We have seen a renewed policing of women's bodies under the
guise of morality or religion from Somalia to Guatemala, Texas
to Haiti. Women have been unjustly condemned by Sharia law
in North Africa, feminists have been deported in Harare under
the pretext of the erosion of family values, women have been
harassed and policed on the streets of Hillbrow, subjected to
virginity testing in rural KwaZulu-Natal, and young lesbians
have been flogged and murdered in Khayelitsha and Mauritius.

In the context of these conservative cultural and sexual beliefs,
it would be very easy for Dr Olivier to blame or pathologise the
complainant's behaviour. Her diagnosis, however, overlooked
healing the complainant's alleged illness and did not address the fact
that when a woman refuses sex, her decision should be respected.
This tacitly endorses crimes against women and children.

Despite Zuma's remarks about African culture and sex, an
African elder was never consulted to verify his statements. This
information was perceived to be of no relevance to the case.
By raising a cultural defence within criminal law, Zuma took
advantage of the cultural pluralism that exists in South Africa.
His intention was to negate the unlawfulness of his act.

Almost all the witnesses, Jacob Zuma, Dr Olivier and Judge Van der Merwe agreed that the complainant was mentally ill. Dr Olivier testified that the complainant could not be believed because she may have an 'encapsulated delusion' or 'an organic pathology, which can be accompanied by hallucinatory images'.[18] She went further to diagnose the complainant with borderline personality disorder.

Listening to the Judge reading Dr Olivier's diagnosis took me back to the time when 'science' was conveniently used as a tool to incarcerate black people in mental hospitals. It also evoked images of black people lying naked on operating tables serving as guinea pigs for 'scientific' experiments in laboratories, hospitals and morgues across the country. Once again, I was reminded of the time when Sarah Baartman was displayed as part of a 'scientific' investigation.

Even though the court diagnosed the complainant's alleged illness, no-one was interested in healing her. The diagnosis was pronounced so as to prove that the complainant's version of events could not be relied upon. Unlike indigenous law, Western justice does not concern itself with mending damaged personal and communal connections. Its main concern is punishment – the harsher, the better.

In a recent outcry about crime in South Africa, many called for improved salaries for police officers, improved investigation and prosecution, clamping down on bribery, etc. Criminologists say we should reclaim our streets through neighbourhood watch patrols and visible policing. While they may be necessary, these suggestions view safety and security as a means of protecting humans from external harm. We also need an internal process to build people's capacities to live their lives in the best possible economic, cultural and spiritual ways in order to render crime unnecessary.

Taking a tough stance on crime should not only be about punishment and imprisonment. We know from statistics that most people in prison are black, and it follows that black families are most affected by the government's tough stance on crime. Surely healing the moral and spiritual wounds in our communities is as critical as sending a clear message to criminals that crime does not pay?

In an interview with Ike Phaahla on SAFM the day after his corruption case was struck off the court's roll, Jacob Zuma was asked if he was going to take legal action against the National Prosecuting Authority for abuse of power. Zuma explained that such an action would be ill advised because the most important intervention was to right the wrongs of the past few years. Upon being asked how the country could right these wrongs, he said we could do so by making sure that the criminal justice system functions effectively.

The interview left me with unanswered questions: what role, if any, does moral justice play in ensuring effective functioning of the criminal justice system in post-apartheid society? In what ways can we inculcate and monitor moral justice? Is there room for African indigenous jurisprudence?

Bridging the cultural divide: indigenous law and transformation within the judiciary in South Africa

Like many other post-colonial nations, South Africa has inherited a dual justice system, with one part based on Western justice and the other based on an indigenous model of justice. With the advent of democracy, a new Constitution gave full recognition to customary law and guaranteed every person the right to participate in a cultural life of his or her choice. The inclusive Constitution called for a re-negotiation of old relationships and the emergence of new ones. These relationships affect every aspect of our society including education, health and the workplace.

According to Thandabantu Nhlapo, of all these negotiated relationships the ones that have ethnicity or culture at their centre are the ones that suffer most from the legacy of the past.[19]

In his view, African customary law remains doubly vulnerable because not only is it required to re-negotiate its content, it also has to re-negotiate the political relationship between itself and the rest of the legal system. This re-negotiation, he argues, occurs against the backdrop of a dominant legal system and a dominant culture whose relationship with African culture has been negative in the past.[20]

Over a decade after the advent of democracy South Africa has yet to come to grips with healing the divide between the Western notion of retributive justice and the African concept of restorative justice. As far as the administration of justice is concerned, a common practice remains one that upholds ideas that reflect the classic Western approach with its sole focus on adjudication and punishment, as opposed to the African approach that concerns itself with notions of healing, forgiveness and the restoration of damaged relationships at individual, family and community levels. This means that Africans are still judged on the basis of the laws that are not in harmony with the ways in which their communities (and life philosophies) are structured.

This situation is not unique to Africa. It is a phenomenon that is experienced by First Nations of the world in Asia, the Americas and the Pacific. In her paper 'Indigenous Justice Systems and Tribal Society', Ada Pecos Melton distinguishes between the practice of indigenous and that of Western law in America.[21] Western law, she asserts, is rooted in a European world-view that is not only hierarchical and adversarial in nature but guided by written laws that limit decision-making powers to very few people.

In this system, two parties are brought into the same room not to generate dialogue, but as adversaries to determine the defendant's guilt or innocence. To achieve this, evidence is often acquired and presented in the most raw and shocking manner. I find it interesting that Advocate Kemp J. Kemp was more than delighted to produce a private manuscript acquired through dubious means as evidence to show that the complainant was an unreliable witness, yet he refused the State's request for permission to use the material acquired from the raids of Zuma's office and other properties. He considered it acceptable and unquestionable to use individuals named in the private unpublished manuscript as witnesses against the complainant. Of particular interest is that Kemp J. Kemp refused to view this invasion of a private emotional space in the same serious light as the invasion of a physical space.

Because the overall objective of Western justice is not to remedy the problem but to punish the offender, the truth is not reached voluntarily and willingly. A legal practitioner becomes like a dentist extracting a tooth without anaesthesia, hoping the pain will become so unbearable that the accuser will ultimately give in and the inconsistencies of his or her story will be exposed. In the event of such a slip, the defence then goes for the kill.

In some cases a lawyer may advise the client that the case against them is 'rock solid' and that a guilty plea will result in a lesser sentence. However, Rupert Ross argues in his book *Returning to the Teachings* that in such circumstances an admission of guilt is not the same as accepting the wrongness of the offence and the hurt it has caused others.[22]

This could explain why many people end up serving their full sentences only to be released from prison still hiding behind lies, excuses and justifications for their deeds. Surrounded by prison authorities and offenders who are also drowning in a sea of lies and deceit, individual offenders are tacitly given permission to deny their moral and spiritual dimensions. An inability to access these dimensions is a form of death.

There is a common saying in Setswana – *letswalo le le phelang ke modisa wa gago*, which means that an active conscience provides a basis for effective policing in our private and sacred spaces; it helps us to make life-enhancing choices. So many of us, rich or poor, are dead while we are alive; we no longer have a conscience. Humans who are unable to feel their own pain cannot take responsibility for the pain they cause to others. Similarly, anyone who cannot feel cannot heal.

This then raises a critical question: in what ways can the justice system bring about healing of individuals, families and communities? Questions of justice in Western societies are relegated to the legal institutions while matters pertaining to morality, forgiveness and reconciliation are left to religion and philosophy. In contrast, indigenous law sees the human being holistically integrated into all sectors of society.

If we hand over our entire lives to the practice of law in Western courts as we are currently doing, how do we envisage reconnecting with other dimensions in our existence? Does the justice system have the orientation, willingness and capacity to practise justice as healing? What role, if any, can indigenous justice play in healing a country ravaged by moral and spiritual breakdown?

Indigenous justice is based on a holistic philosophy founded on a circle of healing for which the main goal is connecting those affected by a specific crime. Unlike in the Western justice system, law is a way of life and justice is an important part of that life. This means that the process of law-making and the administration of justice are an integral part of a socialisation where the young are introduced to the socio-cultural, religious, economic and philosophical realms of life in a village by their elders. The process of law-making and the administration of justice are not guided by written rules but passed on orally from one generation to the other by a council of elders, in which every man in the community has the right to participate. While this process excluded women in the past, the new dispensation has brought with it opportunities for women to provide leadership not only in the home but in the broader community.

In his book *The Healing Wisdom of Africa*, Malidoma Patrice Somé points out that an elder is one whom the village acknowledges as having reached old age as well as an age of maturity and wisdom.

'Elders are repositories of tribal knowledge and life experience, essential resources for the survival of the village, anchoring it firmly to the living foundation of tradition. The old and the elder are the most revered members of the village community and its greatest preservers and nurturers... The elder is as important in the community as the newborn, in that they both share a proximity with the Other world, the ancestors' world.'[23]

In their role as preservers of the community, elders perform functions that include attending to emotional situations in the village, making sure that the laws of the ancestors are not broken, and leading rituals and healing ceremonies. An elder entrusted with these responsibilities is essentially a keeper of a shrine that, like an altar, is a place where one goes to enter into communication with the Other world. Elders play critical roles in ensuring balance and harmony in the community, and the recognition of each elder is carefully debated because it is believed that power in the hands of those who are old but unwise can be lethal.[24]

The involvement of elders in the administration of justice is documented in legal reports from countries such as Australia and Canada. The Murri Court falls within the jurisdiction of the Queensland Magistrate's Court and serves offenders of Aboriginal or Torres Strait Island descent. The Murri Court has a dedicated slot in the court's list of proceedings and its proceedings are held in an inclusive manner for non-English-speaking participants. Often, the magistrate may choose not to wear his or her robes and may sit on the floor at a custom-made oval table that represents a healing circle.[25]

The court comprises community justice groups, which are partially funded by the state and whose members are taken from the local community, the elders' committee and the Community

Corrections Office. According to Magistrate Hennessy, the positive interaction between the participants represents a holistic approach to an historically difficult problem characterised by the representation of Aboriginal people as offenders and white Australians as those who decide on the fate of the offenders.[26]

The aim of the elders in the Murri Court, and in many other indigenous justice systems, is to condemn the offending behaviour in the strongest terms and to teach the community about indigenous philosophies and justice. The acknowledgement of the elders' authority as moral guardians over society is critical for the healing of a community suffering from years of racial oppression and cultural repression. The court's work is not just about finalising a case. It encompasses the reintegration of restorative ideas into existing Western justice procedures.

From the above it is clear that in the indigenous realm, law cannot be separated from morality and spirituality. Cleansing your soul is seen as one of the key elements of ensuring justice and balance. In the court described above, symbols such as indigenous paintings, a message stick and conch shell are displayed prominently in the courtroom to serve as a means of non-verbal communication and to instil a sense of pride and belonging for participants from affected communities. It is believed that people who are not in touch with their life-force are prone to committing atrocities against themselves and others. Efforts aimed at addressing widespread spiritual disconnection are critical in a crime prevention strategy. Crime is also perceived as a human error that requires corrective intervention from families, the community and elders. To correct such wrongs, the offender is expected to show remorse by making a public apology as well as by engaging in public and private acts that demonstrate a commitment to making things right. This means that within indigenous law the offender is given a chance to heal and change.

By giving an offender a chance to heal, the indigenous

system shames the act and not the person.[27] In the case of Jacob Zuma, respect for him as an individual who has contributed significantly to the liberation of the country would be preserved in this system. However, he would still be expected to take full responsibility for his actions.

The day after his acquittal, Zuma apologised for not using a condom in what he termed consensual sex. He did not apologise for being unfaithful to his wives. Because Western law focuses on the offence and not on the broader impact of an offender's acts on his family and community, we will never know how his wives suffered during the rape trial. They will not speak out because 'culture does not allow it'. Inspired by Margaret Singana's 'Stand by your man' and the societal notion of how a married woman should behave, Zuma's wives will be expected to stand firm behind their man, carrying their burdens in silence like good women. After all, *lebitla la mosadi ke bogadi* (once married, a woman must not return to her original family until death, she belongs to her in-laws and must be buried by them).

Within the indigenous justice system, respect is extended not only to the offender but to everyone who has been affected by the conflict. This means that respect for Jacob Zuma would translate into equal respect for President Mbeki who did not deserve to be at the receiving end of acts of disrespect from Zuma's supporters who, among other things, hurled profanities at Mbeki, turning our mother tongue into a traditional weapon of mass destruction. Similarly, others who took a principled stand against Zuma's actions – Barney Pityana, Njabulo Ndebele and Archbishop Tutu – would also be extended respect in terms of this rule.

Finally, one critical element of the system is focusing on the victim to encourage healing at physical, emotional, mental and spiritual levels. Apart from the support offered by women and men outside the court, the complainant was essentially alone. Her voice is almost erased in our hearts as we become like the citizens of Hamelin following the piper from one rendition of *Umshini wam* to another.

In conclusion, allow me to ask a question that continues to haunt me: what lessons, if any, have we learnt from Jacob Zuma's rape trial other than the fact that the abuse of sexual power does not seem to have any serious consequences in South Africa?

The drama of Zuma's rape trial happened in a country ravaged by violent crime, inhumane levels of poverty, an alarming prevalence of HIV/Aids, an ever-increasing number of orphans raising themselves, poor black matric results, poor service delivery from government departments, alcohol, drugs and other addictions, an increasing prevalence of cancer, the emergence of a new drug-resistant strain of TB, high divorce rates and tension in intimate relationships, teenage pregnancies, mothers dying during childbirth, young women seduced by the commercial power of prostitution, middle-class parents leaving their children to be raised by DSTV while they chase deals and deadlines, white farmers killed with impunity... I could go on and on. However, I refuse to be buried in a heap of apathy and hopelessness.

In the past decade South Africa had made incredible progress against immense odds. If we focus our undivided attention on ongoing collective political and socio-economic challenges, we cannot be held hostage by one man's inability to act appropriately as an elder and leader.

It is very clear that the justice system as it is currently applied has had no impact on awakening the nation from its moral and spiritual stupor. Despite tough sentences and a prison system bursting at the seams, our hearts and minds are numb to rage and pain. It has therefore become critical at this point in our evolution as a democracy that we counter the cruelty of our times by honouring a spiritual connection between one human being and another. An African elder, Eskia Mphahlele, has this to say:

'When we track down and kill another person or
persons, we ourselves individually die some. We place
the best in ourselves – the human spirit, otherwise
called God – in unspeakable jeopardy.' [28]

For me, the Zuma rape trial did not help relieve the fear
that I will not be able to protect myself and my daughter or
her daughter from rape. Since I started working in the area
of gender-based violence, I have carried a fear of being raped.
When I lie awake at night after watching a news bulletin riddled
with bullets and blood, rage and rape, I long for a place where
women and children are cherished and loved by equally loved
and self-loving men.

Speaking of love, Leo Buscaglia defines it as the only word
which is big enough to engulf all of life. If we miss out on love,
he says, we die a little and miss out on life.[29] How, then, do we
learn to love and to live?

As we set out in search of our shrines, allow me to end this
journey with an excerpt from Mazisi Kunene's poem 'The
Ancestors and the Sacred Mountain', quoted by Eskia Mphahlele
in his address at the opening of an exhibition at the Local History
Museum in Durban:[30]

'People must move without fear
Nor should they raise their voices to the hurricanes
But must with their power command them to silence.
It is us, the descendants of the lions
Who must rule, without us the earth itself would end.'

Endnotes

Silence is not an option

1   Watson, R.L. 'Abolition, violence and rape. 'Thoughts on the post-emancipation experiences of the United States and the Cape Colony'. *The Journal of South African and American Studies*, Issue 22, April 2006.

2   Davidson, Gordon & McLaughlin, Corinne. 1994. *Spiritual Politics: Changing the world from inside out*. New York: Ballantine Books.

3   Pityana, Barney. 'Leadership is more than just singing'. Second JD Baqwa Memorial Lecture, 2006. *City Press*, 13 August 2006.

4   Koka, Ntate Kgalushi. 2001. *Current Perspectives on Afrikan Philosophy – Ubuntu/ Botho*. Johannesburg: Kara Heritage Institute.

5   Mp hahlele, Eskia. 2004. *ESKIA Continued*. Johannesburg: Stainbank and Associates.

6   Op cit

7   Motsei, Mmatshilo. 2004. *Hearing Visions Seeing Voices*. Johannesburg: Jacana Media.

8   Deputy President Jacob Zuma. Address at the first Moral Regeneration Movement Conference at Eskom Conference Centre, Midrand, November 2004. Conference held two years after the launch of MRM at Waterkloof Air Base, Pretoria on 18 April 2002.

9   Deputy President Jacob Zuma. Address on the occasion of World Aids Day, Athlone Stadium, Cape Town, 1 December 2004.

10 Welsing, Frances Cress. 1999. *The Isis Papers – The Keys to the Colors*. Chicago: Third World Press, p. 81.

11 Ibid

12 Ngcobo, Lauretta. 1999. *And They Didn't Die*. Pietermaritzburg: University of Natal Press.

13 Personal communication with a rape survivor.

14 Reference made to a statement made by the complainant in Jacob Zuma's trial.

15 Griffin, Susan. 'Rape: The All American Crime'. In Angela Davis. 1990. *Women, Culture and Politics*. New York: Vintage Books, pp. 39–40.

16 Ya Salaam, Kalamu. 'Rape: A radical analysis from an African–American perspective'. *ChickenBones: A Journal for Literary and Artistic African-American Themes*. www.nathanielturner.com/raperadicalanalysis.htm Accessed 2006/05/05

17 Complete illiteracy – being unable to read or write. Functional illiteracy – being unable to function in a modern world due to poor reading and writing skills. Aliteracy – being able to read but choosing not to read. Figures quoted by Elinor Sisulu. 'The culture of reading and the book chain: How do we achieve a quantum leap?' Keynote address, Symposium on the cost of a culture for reading, Centre for the Book, Cape Town, 16–17 September 2004.

18 Op cit

19 Ibid

20 Abrahams, Yvette. 'Colonialism, dysfunction and disjuncture: Sarah Baartmann's resistance (remix)'. *Agenda* no. 23, 2003, pp. 12–26.

21 Davis, Angela. 'Rape, racism and the capitalist setting'. *The Black Scholar.* November–December 1981.

22 Ibid

23 Lewis, Desiree. Editorial. *Feminist Africa*: Issue 2, 2003.

24 Steve Biko quoted in Abrahams. *Agenda* no. 23, 2003, p. 12.

25 Bynoe, Yvonne. 'Defining the female image through rap music and hip hop culture'. *Doula: The Journal of Rap Music and Hip Hop Culture.* Volume 1, Issue 2, Winter 2001.

26 Tabane, Rapule & Sokupa, Vuyo. 'Sex pest Goniwe booted out of ANC'. *Mail and Guardian*, 15–20 December 2006.

27 Ibid

28 Lewis, Rudolph. 'Feminism, Black Erotica and Revolutionary Love'. *Chickenbones: A Journal for Literary and Artistic African-American Themes.* www. nathanielturner.com Accessed 2006/03/19.

War against women

1 Dworkin, A. 1980. 'Pornography and Grief'. In Lederer, L. (ed.) *Take back the night: women on Pornography.* New York, William Morrow and Co, Inc. p287.

2 Heise, LL., Pitanguy, A., Germaine, A. 1994. *Violence against women: The hidden health burden.* Washington DC The World Bank.

3 Genesis 30:20. *The Bible.* New King James Version.

4 Emecheta, Buchi. 1980. *The Joys of Motherhood.* African Writers Series no. 227. London: Heinemann.

5 Bunch, C. 1992. *Overview of violence against women.* New York: Ford Foundation Women's Program Forum.

6 The State of Food Insecurity in the World. FAO Report, 2005.

7 Female infanticide. www.gendercide.org

8 UN Report of the Special Rapporteur on Violence against women, its causes and consequences submitted in accordance with the Commission on Human Rights resolution 2001/49.

9   Ibid

10   Dowry in India. www.indianchild.com/dowry Accessed 2006/04/21

11   Ibid

12   'Tanzania: Study links payment of bride price to abuse of women. IRIN news.org 2 June 2006.

13   Hassan, Yasmeen. 'The Fate of Pakistani Women'. *International Herald Tribune*, 25 May 1999.

14   'Honor killings still plague Turkish Province'. *The Toronto Star*, 14 May 1998.

15   'Honour killings now seen as murder'. *The Sydney Morning Herald*, 24 April 2000.

16   Imam, A.M. Women's reproductive and sexual rights and the offence of Zina in Muslim laws in Nigeria. www.pambazuka.org

17   'Iraq: Decades of Suffering, now women deserve better'. Amnesty International report, February 2005.

18   UNICEF. Child Protection – female genital mutilation. www.unicef.org/protection/index_genitalmutilation.hmtl.

19   Op cit

20   Ibid

21   McLean, S. & Graham, S. *Female circumcision, excision and infibulation: the facts and proposals for change.* London: The Minority Rights Group Report, no. 47.

22   Ibid

23   Ibid

24   El-Saadawi, Nawal. 1980. *The Hidden Face of Eve: Women in the Arab World.* London: Zed Press.

25   Personal communication with a physically abused woman.

26   Klugman, B. 'The politics of contraception in South Africa'. Women's Studies Int. Forum 1990, 13(3): 261–271.

27   Brown, Julia. 'The late apartheid's state's search for a racially-specific immunological contraceptive'. Paper based on research conducted for author's MA thesis 'The End of the Future: The Development of the South African Chemical and Biological Weapons Research Programme, 1981–1991'. University of Natal, Durban, 2002.

28   Ibid

29   Gendercide watch: maternal mortality. www.gendercide.org/case_maternal.html

30   Jacobson, JL. 'Women's reproductive health: the silent emergency'. Washington DC, World Watch Paper 102, June 1991.

31   Sooka, Bhavna. 'High-level talks after 26 "sex-slave" arrests'. www.iol.co.za/general/news/newsprint.php Accessed 2006/12/22

32   Savides, Matthew & Mchunu, Noloyiso. 'Police to discuss sex slave probe'. www.iol.co.za/general/news/newsprint.php Accessed 2006/12/22

33   Op cit

34   Ibid
35   Madslien, Jorn. 'Sex trade's reliance on forced labour'. *BBC News*, 12 May 2005. http://news.bbc.co.uk/1/hi/business/4532617.stm accessed 31 May2006.
36   Bindel, Julie. 'World Cup sex slave fears'. *Mail and Guardian*, 2–8 June 2006.
37   Ibid

War on sexual terror: a woman's body as a site for battle
1   In Davis, Angela. 1990. *Women, Culture and Politics*. New York: Vintage Books.
2   Makatile, Don. 'Rollicking, roaring Zuma circus becomes the hottest show in town'. *Sunday World*, 19 March 2006.
3   'Shattered Lives: The Case for Tough International Arms Control'. Amnesty International and Oxfam International, 2003.
4   Ibid
5   'The Impact of Guns on Women's Lives'. Amnesty International: The International Action Network on Small Arms and Oxfam International, 2005.
6   Keitetsi, China. 2002. *Child Soldier: Fighting for My Life*. Johannesburg: Jacana Media.
7   In 'Lives Blown Apart: Crimes Against Women in Times of Conflict – Stop Violence against Women'. Amnesty International Report 2004.
8   Alfredson, Lisa. 2001. *Sexual exploitation of child soldiers: an exploration and analysis of global dimensions and trends*. Coalition to stop the use of child soldiers, p. 5.
9   Ciabattari, Jane. 'While Cruel Wars Rage, African Women Wage Peace'. Women's eNews, 15 March 2006.
10   Op cit
11   Ibid
12   Eliseev, Alex & Cherney, Mike. 'Jealousy and rejection sparked bloody massacre'. *The Star*, 5 April 2006.
13   Thompson, JH. 2006. *An Unpopular War. From Afkak to Bosbefok*. Cape Town: Zebra Press.
14   Keen, Sam. 1992. *Fire in the Belly: On Being a Man*. New York: Bantam Books.
15   Ndebele, Njabulo. 'Why Zuma's bravado is brutalizing the public'. *Sunday Times*, 5 March 2006.
16   Masondo, Amos. 'Zuma saga analysis uses quackery, resulting in a total misdiagnosis'. *Sunday Times*, 12 March 2006.
17   Sankara, Thomas. 1990. *Women's Liberation and the African Freedom Struggle*. New York: Pathfinder Press, p. 11.
18   Op cit
19   'UN welcomes life sentences on soldiers accused of massive rape'. UN News Service, 13 April 2006. www.allafrica.com

20 Op cit
21 'Iraq: Decades of suffering now women deserve better'. Amnesty International Report, 22 February 2005.
22 Laurence, Charles. 'The rape that shames America'. *The Star*, 27 November 2006, p. 15.
23 Grant, Linda. 'The Rubble Women'. *The Guardian Review*. 2 July 2005, p. 9.
24 'Neither blood nor rape for oil'. Black Women's Rape Action Project and Women against Rape, 12 May 2004.
25 Ibid
26 Fairweather, Eileen *et al.* 1984. 'Only the Rivers Run Free: Northern Ireland, The Women's War'. *Pluto Press*, London.
27 Cock, Jacklyn. 'Feminism and Militarism: Some questions raised by the Gulf War'. *South African Defence Review*, issue no. 6, 1992.
28 Shabi, Rachel. 'The fight not to fight'. *Mail and Guardian*, 21–27 April 2006.
29 Ibid
30 Op cit
31 Ibid
32 Tambo, OR. Speech at the concluding session of the conference of the Women's Section of the ANC, Luanda, Angola, 14 September 1981.
33 Ibid p. 1–2
34 Nyoka, Mtutuzeli. 2004. *I Speak to the Silent*. Pietermaritzburg: University of KwaZulu-Natal Press, pp. 177–178.
35 Malefane, Moipone. 'Women were "sex objects" in ANC exile camps'. *Sunday Times*, 3 March 2006.
36 Ibid
37 Williams, Karen. 'Rape is a weapon of war'. *The Mercury*, 9 November 2005.
38 Motsei, Mmatshilo. 2003. *Sacred rocks, Ancient Voices. Spiritual Significance of a Rock and Water in African Healing*. Unpublished report commissioned by the Freedom Park Trust.
39 'No Woman, No World'. *True Love* magazine, August 2006.
40 In Davis, Angela. 1990. *Women, Culture and Politics*. New York: Vintage Books.
41 Enloe, Cynthia. 1983. *Does the Khaki Become You? The Militarization of Women's Lives*. New York: Pluto Press
42 Matsui, Yayori. 'Women and armed conflict – foreign military bases as a source of violence against women'. www.aworc.org/bpfa/gov/escap/vaww.hmtl. Accessed 20/05/2006.
43 'Decades of impunity: serious allegations of rape of Kenyan women by UK army personnel'. Amnesty International Report, 2 July 2003.
44 Ibid
45 'Foreign Press Lambasts South Africa'. *Sunday Times* Foreign Desk, 14 May 2006.

46   Maughan, Karyn. 'Sex-Mad Troops'. *Saturday Star,* 4 November 2006.

47   Ibid

48   Pilger, John. 2002. *The New Rulers of the World.* London, New York: Verso.

49   Ibid

50   Ibid

Lucifer, deliver us from evil

1   Quoted in White, Evelyn C. 1985. *Chain Chain Change. For black women dealing with physical and emotional abuse.* Washington, Seattle: The Seal Press.

2   Mbalula, Fikile. 'Zuma support is no sycophantic ramble'. www.anc.org.za/youth. Accessed 2006/06/14.

3   Ibid

4   In Keen, Sam. 1992. *Fire in the Belly: On being a man.* New York: Bantam Books.

5   Swart, Werner. 'She's a devil'. Outrage as ANCYL labels the accuser as Lucifer. *The Citizen,* 12 May 2006.

6   Mbalula, Fikile. 'Zuma support is no sycophantic ramble'. www.anc.org.za/youth/ Accessed 2006/06/14

7   *Holy Bible.* New King James version.

8   Bratcher, Dennis. 'Lucifer in Isaiah 14:12–17, Translation and Ideology'. The Voice. Biblican and Theological Resources for Growing Christians. www.cresourcei.org/lucifer.html. Accessed 2006/05/31.

9   From Wikipedia. www.wikipedia.org/wiki/Lucifer. Accessed 2006/05/31.

10   Taken from the Catholic Encyclopedia. www.newadvent.org. Accessed 2006/05/31.

11   Mtintso, Thenjiwe. 'From "swart gevaar" to "vrou gevaar"'. *Mail and Guardian,* 11–17 August 2006, p. 23.

12   Esack, Faried. The *Unfinished Business of a Liberation Struggle.* Paper presented at the Central Methodist Church, Johannesburg. 13 September 1986.

13   Malefane, M, & Mafela, N. 'And now for the judgement'. *Sunday Times,* 7 May 2006.

14   www.int.iol.co.za\Church youth sexually active 10 February 2006. Accessed 2006/07/12.

15   Ibid

16   Tracy, Steven R. 2005. *Mending the Soul. Understanding and healing abuse.* Michigan: Zondervan.

17   De Beauvoir, Simone. 'The Second Sex'. In Northrup, Dr Christiane. 1998. *Women's Bodies Women's Wisdom.* London: Piatkus, p. 5

18   Op cit

19   Smith, Krystyna. *Rape of the Soul.* www.speakout.org.za/survivors/religion/religion_rape_of_the_soul.hmtl. Accessed 2006/05/28.

Endnotes

20 Simmermacher, Gunther. 'Church under attack?' *Southern Cross*, June 2003. In www.speakout.org.za/survivors/religion/religion_the_sa_catholic.html. Accessed 2006/06/28.

21 The Vatican and Violence against Women. 47th Session of the Commission on the Status of Women. Church Centre, New York. 12 March 2003.

22 Ibid

23 Ibid

24 Ibid

25 Personal communication with an abused woman.

26 Proverbs 6:23–26. *Holy Bible*. New King James version.

27 Amanze, Rev. Dr James. 1998. *African Christianity in Botswana: The case of African Independent Churches*. Gweru: Mambo Press.

28 Ibid

29 www.DACB.org The Dictionary of African Christian Biography. Accessed 2006/05/22.

30 Op cit

31 Ibid

32 www.pzadmin.pitzer.edu/masilela/newafrre/maxeke/maxekeS.htm. Accessed 2006/07/12.

33 Phiri, Isabel. 'African Women's Theologies in the New Millennium.' *Agenda* 61 2004, pp. 16–24.

34 Stewart, Iris J.. 'Religion, Rape and War.' www.awakenedwoman.com/stewart_rape.htm. Accessed 2006/06/28.

35 Numbers 31:7–18. *Holy Bible*, New King James version.

36 Smith, Charlene. 'Virgin rape myth: a media creation or a clash between myth and a lack of HIV treatment?' Academic paper, Sex and Secrecy Conference, Wits University, 2003.

37 Genesis 19: 4–8. *Holy Bible*. New King James version.

38 Molele, Charles, Malefane, Moipone & Mafela, Ndivhuho. 'The world according to Jacob Zuma'. *Sunday Times*, 9 April 2006.

39 Phiri, Isabel. 'Weddings and Lobola'. In Adeyemo, Tokunboh (ed.) 2006. *Africa Bible Commentary*. Nairobi: WorldAlive Publishers, p. 799.

40 Phiri, Isabel. 'The Bible and Polygamy'. In Adeyemo. *Africa Bible Commentary*.

41 Okorocha, Eunice. 'Cultural Issues and the Biblical Message'. In Adeyemo.

42 West, Gerald, Zondi-Mabizela, Phumzile, Maluleke, Martin, Khumalo, Happiness , Matsepe, Smadz & Naidoo, Mirolyn. 'Rape in the House of David: The Biblical story of Tamar as a Resource for Transformation'. *Agenda* 61, 2004. pp. 36–41.

43 Ngewa, Samuel. 'What is the Church?' In Ademeyo. *African Bible Commentary*t.

44 Biko, Steve. 2005. *I Write What I like*. Johannesburg: Picador Africa, pp. 104–105.

45 Northrup, Dr Christiane. 1998. *Women's Bodies Women's Wisdom*. London: Piatkus, p. 575.

46 In Magesa, Laurenti. Christology, African Women and Ministry. www.sedos.org/english/magesa. Accessed 2006/05/29.

47 Rape and Religion, Beloved of God. www.speakout.org.za/survivors/religion Accessed 2006/06/28.

Burn the bitch

1   Tolsi, Niren, Sosibo, Kwanele Makgetla, Tumi & Dibetle, Monako. 'This mama is speaking lies'. *Mail and Guardian*, 24–30 March 2006.

2   The Rich List. *Sunday Times*. 6 August 2006.

3   Ibid

4   McCall, Nathan. 1994. *Makes Me Wanna Holler: A Young Black Man in America*. New York: Vintage Books.

5   Quoted in Carroll, Rebecca. 1995 .*Swing Low: Black men writing*. New York: Crown Trade Paperbacks.

6   www.thugz-network.com. Accessed 2006/07/08.

7   'Hip Hop 101'. Music review by Luke Bobo. www.ransomfellowship.org/Music Accessed 2006/07/08.

8   Jeff Chang interviewed by Oliver Wang. www.cantstopwontstop.com. Accessed 2006/07/20.

9   Ya Salaam, Kalamu. 'It Didn't Jes Grew: The Social and Aesthetic Significance of African American Music'. *African American Review* 29(2) 1995, pp351–375.

10 Bynoe, Yvonne. 'Defining the female image through rap music and hip hop'. *DOULA: The Journal of Rap Music and Hip Hop Culture*, Volume 1, Issue 2, Winter 2001, pp21–24.

11 Op cit

12 Ibid

13 Op cit

14 Tate, Greg. 'Hip Hop Turns 30: Whatcha celebratin for'? *The Village Voice*. www.villagevoice.com Accessed 2006/07/21.

15 Ibid

16 James, Darryl. 'The Dis Factor'. www.rapsheet.com Accessed 2006/07/08.

17 Kennedy, Lauren. 'Music, Social Justice and Market Manipulations: An Interview with Tricia Rose'. www.triciarose.com/commentary.shtml Accessed 2006/07/08.

18 Mogoatlhe, Lerato. 'On the Down Low'. *City Press – City Pulse*, 6 August 2006.

19 Armstrong, Edward G. 'Gangsta Misogyny: A content analysis of the portrayal of violence against women in rap music, 1987–1993'. *Journal of Criminal Justice and Popular Culture*, 8(2) 2001, pp 96–126.

20 Ibid

21 In Thompson, Carla. 'Hip-hop women recount their abuse at their own risk'. WeNews correspondent. www.womensnews.org/article.cfm/dyn/aid/2775/context/cover. Accessed 2006/07/08.

22 Esack, Faried. 'What do men stand to gain from gender equality?' In Motsei, M. (ed.) *Name the pain, face the shame. Men as part of the solution to violence against women*. Unpublished manuscript.

23 Ngwenya, Bongani. '*Sika lekhekhe* off the air'. www.inkundla.net/indaba/2005/Mpandula/sika/php Accessed 2006/11/20

24 hooks, bell. 'Sexism and Misogyny: Who takes the rap? Misogyny, gangsta rap and The Piano'. www.race.eserver.org/misogyny.html Accessed 2006/07/27.

25 Ibid

26 Generation Next Youth Brand Survey. *The Sunday Times* in association with Monash South Africa. *The Sunday Times* supplement, 30 July 2006.

27 Ayanna. 'The exploitation of women in hip-hop culture'. My Sistahs – a project from Advocates for Youth. www.mysistas.org/features/hiphop.htm Accessed 2006/07/08.

28 Kabomo. 'Life as Kelly Khumalo'. *Y-Mag*, Aug/Sept 2006.

29 Ibid

30 In Taylor, Allana. 'Writing to Survive. A Look at bell hooks'. www.penn-partners.org. Accessed 2006/07/27.

31 Sibiya, Gugu. 'Mshoza does vanishing act as wild drug-abuse stories do the rounds'. *Sowetan*, 11 July 2006 .

32 Op cit

33 Op cit

34 Ibid

35 Ward, Kelly. 'Back That Ass Up: A Discussion of Black Women in Rap'. www.gwu.edu. Accessed 2006/07/08.

36 Khumalo, Sipho. 'Fans celebrate their hero's victory'. *Pretoria News*, 21 September 2006.

37 The Hammer of Witches. Quoted in case study: 'The European Witch-Hunts, c.1450–1750'. www.gendercide.org/case_witchhunts.html Accessed 2006/05/21.

38 Ferguson, Ann. Review of Silvia Federici's *Caliban and the Witch: Women, the Body and Primitive Accumulation*. (2005, Autonomedia, NYC). In *Wagadu – a Journal of Transnational Women's and Gender Studies*. http://web.cortland.edu/wagadu. Accessed 2006/06/20.

39 Mbowane, Pinkie. 'Safety at stake over witchcraft accusations. A commentary'. *Sowetan*, 31 March 1999.

40 Badoe, Yaba. 'What makes a woman a witch'? *Feminist Africa* issue 5, 2005.

41 Ibid

42 Stuart Jefferies, 'The Mother of all Insults'. *The Guardian*, 12 July 2006.

'Women ask for it': from kangaroo court to kanga court

1 Tolsi, Niren, Sosibo, Kwanele, Makgetla, Tumi & Dibetle, Monako. 'This mama is speaking lies'. *Mail and Guardian*, 24–30 March 2006.

2 Maughan, Karyn & Gifford, Gill. 'Discovering the complainant's mindset "vital"'. *The Star*, 27 April 2006.

3 Aidoo, Ama Ata. 'To Be a Woman'. In Rorbin Morgan. (ed.) 1984. *Sisterhood is Global*. New York: Penguin Books.

4 www.powa.htm. Accessed 2006/04/22.

5 Ya Salaam, Kalamu. 'Debunking the myths'. *Chickenbones: A Journal for Literary and Artistic African-American Themes.* www.nathanielturner.com/debunkingmythskys.htm. Accessed 2006/03/19.

6 Ibid

7 Cavanagh, Dawn & Mabele, Prudence. 'I was raped and I am sane'. *City Press*, 14 May 2006.

8 Malala, Justice. 'Media buys into miniskirt myth'. *Sunday Times*, 19 March 2006.

9 www.glcom./hassan/kanga_history.html. Accessed 2006/04/20.

10 Ibid

11 Lekota, Ida. 'This is how you cast your vote'. *Sowetan*, 10 October 2006.

12 Conversation. Desiree Lewis talks to Molara Ogundipe, leading feminist theorist, poet, literary critic, educator and activist about the interface of politics, culture and education. AGI–GWS E-journal launch issue. Feminist Africa_files\morala6.htm. Accessed 2006/04/12.

13 Ibid

14 In Motsei, Mmatshilo. (ed.) *Name the pain, face the shame: Men as part of the solution to violence against women*. Unpublished manuscript.

15 Rantao, Jovial. 'Women's attitude to rape is on trial'. *The Star,* 10 March 2006.

16 Somé, Malidoma Patrice. 1999. *The Healing Wisdom of Africa*. New York: Penguin Putnam Inc.

17 Ibid

18 Ibid

19 Meintjies, Frank. 'Redefining masculinity in a changing world'. In Motsei, Mmatshilo. (ed.) *Name the pain, face the shame: Men as part of the solution to violence against women*. Unpublished manuscript.

20 Ibid

21 Meloche, Maureen K. In *Le Mieux-Etre Wellness Newsletter.* Undated.

22 Nkululeko, Dabi. 'The Right to Self-Determination in Research: Azania and Azanian Women'. In Qunta, Christine. (ed.) 1987. *Women in Southern Africa*. Johannesburg: Skotaville Publishers.

23 Ibid

24 Brown, Karima & Mde, Vukani. 'Zuma and the ANC: When the wheel of fortune turns'. *Business Day*, 10 May 2006.

25 Dowrick, Stephanie.1997. *Forgiveness and Other Acts of Love*. New York: WW Norton and Company.

26 Ibid

27 Ibid

28 McCall. Nathan. 1997. 'Men: We just don't get it'. In *What's Going On*. New York: Vintage Books, pp. 27–28.

29 Ibid

30 hooks, bell. 2004. *The Will to Change: Men, Masculinity and Love*. New York: Washington Square Press.

31 Jensen, Robert. 'Patriarchal sex'. In Schacht, Steven P. & Ewing, Doris W. (eds.) 1998. *Feminism and Men: Reconstructing Gender Relations*. New York: New York University Press, p. 105.

32 Ibid

33 Mda, Zakes. 'Men's reflections of women and violence'. In Motsei, Mmatshilo. (ed.) *Name the pain face the shame: Men as part of the solution to violence against women*. Unpublished manuscript.

After the verdict, what next? Justice as part of the moral and spiritual healing agenda in South Africa

1 Wa Loate, Sello. 'Violence-related deaths in the lives of young black men in Alexandra township'. In Motsei, Mmatshilo. (ed.) *Name the pain, face the shame: South African men as part of the solution to violence against women*. Unpublished manuscript.

2 Ibid

3 Brown, Karima & Mde, Vukani. 'Zuma and the ANC: When the wheel of fortune turns'. *Business Day*, 10 May 2006.

4 Hoppers, Catherine A. Odora. 2004. *Culture, Indigenous knowledge and development: The role of the university*. Occasional paper no. 5, Johannesburg: Centre for Education Policy Development.

5 Ibid

6 Nmehielle, Vincent O.. 'Cultures within cultures: When laws ignore reality'. *Cultural Survival Quarterly*. Issue 30.1, 27 March 2006.

7 Hotep, Uhuru. 2003. *Decolonizing the African Mind: Further Analysis and Strategy*. Kwame Ture Youth Leadership Institute.

8 Ibid

9 Ibid

10   Armah, Ayi Kwei. 'The identity of the creators of ancient Egypt'. *New African*
     April 2006, pp. 16–20.
11   Ibid
12   Op cit
13   State vs. Jacob Gedleyihlekisa Zuma. High Court of South Africa (Witwatersrand
     Division). 8/5/2006 p. 135.
14   Ibid
15   Maughan, Karyn & Gifford, Gill. 'Zuma "plotted" rape'. *The Star*, 5 April 2006.
16   McFadden, Patricia. 'Sexual pleasure as a feminist choice'. *Feminist Africa*, issue 2,
     2003.
17   Mama, Amina, Pereira, Charmaine & Takyiwaa Manuh. Editorial: Sexual
     Cultures. *Feminist Africa*, issue 2, 2003.
18   Ibid
19   Nhlapo, Thandabantu. 'The judicial function of traditional leaders: A contribution
     to restorative justice?' Paper presented at the conference of The Association of Law
     Reform Agencies of Eastern and Southern Africa (ALRAESA). Vineyard Hotel,
     Cape Town 14–17 March 2005.
20   Ibid
21   Melton, Ada Pecos. 'Indigenous justice and tribal society'. Tribal Court
     Clearinghouse. www.tribal-institute.org/articles/melton1.htm. Accessed
     2006/08/17.
22   Ross, Rupert. 1996. *Returning to the Teachings: Exploring Aboriginal Justice.*
     Toronto: Penguin Books.
23   Somé, Malidoma Patrice. 1999. *The Healing Wisdom of Africa: Finding Life
     Purpose through Nature, Ritual and Community.* New York: Penguin Putnam Inc,
     pp. 123–124.
24   Ibid
25   Hennesy, Annette. 'Indigenous Sentencing Practice in Australia'. International
     Society for Reform of Criminal Law Conference, Brisbane, July 2006.
26   Ibid
27   Op cit
28   Mphahlele, Eskia. Address at the exhibition of the local history museum Durban.
     In *ESKIA Continued.* 2004. Johannesburg: Stainbank and Associates, p. 77.
29   Buscaglia, Leo F. 1983. *Living, Loving and Learning.* New York: Fawcett
     Columbine.
30   Op cit